WINES OF
ITALY

"Since, Bacchus, thou art father
Of wines, to thee the rather
We dedicate this cellar . . ."

from Ben Jonson's
The Dedication of the
King's New Cellar to Bacchus

WINES OF ITALY

by

CHARLES G. BODE

DOVER PUBLICATIONS, INC.
NEW YORK

Published in Canada by General Publishing Company, Ltd., 30 Lesmill Road, Don Mills, Toronto,
Ontario.

This Dover edition, first published in 1974, is a
slightly revised republication of the work originally published in 1956 by Peter Owen, Ltd., London and The McBride Company, Inc., New York.
For the present edition the black-and-white illustrations of the original have been deleted and a
map of Italy, p. 8, has been especially prepared.
This Dover edition is published by special arrange-
ment with Peter Owen, Ltd.

International Standard Book Number: 0-486-23003-1
Library of Congress Catalog Card Number: 73-93282

Manufactured in the United States of America
Dover Publications, Inc.
180 Varick Street
New York, N.Y. 10014

CONTENTS

Acknowledgments   7

CHAPTER   PAGE

  I The sunny side of drinking   9

 II Mostly about Chianti   17

III The Wines of Verona   22

 IV South Tyrol   30
     Moscato

  V More Dessert Wines   39
     Sicily and Southern Italy

 VI Marsala   48
     Liqueurs—Brandies—Apéritifs

VII Rome and Naples   56

VIII Asti Spumante   68

 IX The Wines of Piedmont   77

  X Vermouth   86

 XI Liguria   94
     Lombardy
     The Wines of the Emilia-Romagna
     Vin Santo

XII Cooking with Wine   110
     Wine in your Home

Index   121

ACKNOWLEDGMENTS

In the first place I wish to thank my dear friends Riccardo Gatti, Antonio Ghirelli, and Arturo Frontali, whose name may stand in honour of his late father. What I know of Italy, and of her wines, I owe chiefly to their never failing guidance.

My gratitude is due to all those who so generously gave me their valuable time and advice in compiling this book, to Miss Margaret Stevenson, Cavaliere Guglielmo Bertani, Mr. Carlo Mariotti, Mr. Angelo and Mr. Giovanni Parmigiani, Commendatore Carlo Sacchi, Dr. Vittorio Schiazzano, Dr. Richard Teltscher, Mr. Giacinto Trossi, Dr. Attilio Turati, Mr. Owen Walter Wakeling.

I also gratefully acknowledge the assistance given to me by Dr. A. Camurati, Mr. Max Cattabriga, Mr. Ettore Giordano, Mr. Pier Martini, Mr. Harold Marzagalli, Dr. Giovanni Peano, Dr. Gustavo Prada, Conte Rizzardi, Mr. Frederick Albert Roach, Dr. Nicola Di Suni, Mr. A. Tiboni, and Mr. Brandino Vignali.

I am indebted in no lesser way to Mr. Giulio Bollati, Dr. Luciano Foa, Mr. Armando Guglielmi, and Mr. Erich Linder, whose help enabled me to bring this book about.

London, 1956.

I

Se io sono pallido dei miei colori,
non voio dottori,
non voio dottori,
ma vinazza, vinazza,
e fiaschi di vini.
*(When I look pale, I want no doctors, ever,
but wine and wine, and still more of it).*

VENEZIAN-FRIULIAN FOLK RHYME.

Wine in Italy is part of everyman's life. To an Italian, wine is his faithful companion—and not always a boon companion—almost from childhood on through all the joys and vicissitudes the gods may send him. Wine is his comforter in sorrow, his encouraging friend when he feels courage is deserting him, wine is his stimulating or calming "good spirit". A life without wine is something an Italian could hardly imagine—and amazingly there is very little drunkenness in Italy.

It is not easy to get Italian wines, and wine in general for that matter, into proper perspective to the Englishman or American at home. We look upon wine as something to drink on special occasions; to the Italian it is an every day affair even more indispensable than beer, tea, whisky, and perhaps gin are to us. He has a glass of wine with his meals, he has a glass of wine whenever he is thirsty, he has a glass of wine to enliven a casual meeting with a friend, and every Italian housewife swears on her special kind of wine as an infallible remedy against illness.

Every Italian farmer grows his own wine for his own use. In the better years—better either in quantity, or

9

quality, or both—he will store some of it away to allow it to mature, and keep it for a special treat, for a special meal on a special day, or to welcome a much honoured friend . . . "Now just wait a moment, I bring a bottle of the good one", he will say after the first glass of something that is kept handy on the kitchen table or thereabouts has quenched your thirst. Now he wants to sit down with you and have a quiet chat, not having seen you "for such a long time" which may have been ten years, ten months, or ten weeks—sometimes even ten days qualify "for the good one"! And surprisingly enough—considering the clamour made by shippers and connoisseurs alike with German and French vintage charts—these farm wines are in most cases not just drinkable, but really good.

Very frequently (it depends on the district) the ordinary wine will be what the Italians call *vinello*—a "little wine", of low alcohol content: it has perhaps only six or seven per cent (that is about 10° to 12° proof spirit) .* It is of course no quality wine, because sugar content and acidity stand so to speak apart, instead of being integrated as they are in properly matured wine; but it is rather pleasant to drink, very refreshing and not intoxicating: motorists may take a hint!

There is considerable trade going on locally with the cheap *vino del paese*, as the farmers sell their surplus to the cobbler, the workmen, the doctor, and to the inn in the village. These in turn are very proud of their individual suppliers. They are usually faithful to them for years, if not for generations, although on the other hand this does not mean that they do not make an occasional sally into the surrounding country to discover a demijohn

*American readers should note that Mr. Bode uses the British measure of proof spirit, which is established as "that which at the temperature of 51° F. weighs exactly 12/13 of an equal measure of distilled water."

of something special! They will speak of a good wine they had discovered years ago with the same nostalgic enthusiasm an Englishman feels when he describes a cricket match.

Whatever is shipped from one place to another is subject to a Government regulation establishing that its alcohol content must not be less than 10%—that is, 17½ degrees proof spirit. This assures a certain standard minimum quality, as no wine can properly mature if its alcohol content is less. Again, motorists note: there is no law anywhere in the world (not even in England) which would insist that alcoholic "beverages" must be taken in quantity. Italians, during their working day and when they drink for refreshment in the heat, take their wine mixed half and half, or with one third of water, which brings the alcoholic content down to something which will not interfere with their work and would not interfere with your driving either.

So long as you stay at small places, 'do as the Romans do' and drink *il vino del paese*—the local wine. It will vary from district to district, sometimes you will find it better, sometimes not quite so good, but it will always be cheap and will rarely disappoint you. The one exception is the Ligurian Riviera which is really an aggregate of very small places with an overgrown tourist industry. Their vineyards cannot produce a sufficient quantity of good *vino nostrano* for all the thirsty people who spend their holidays swimming, rowing and sunbathing. Besides, the Ligurian coast is in general not very favoured by nature as far as wine-growing is concerned.

When buying or ordering wines originating from out-lying districts, for instance, Piedmont wines in Liguria or Tuscany wines in Lombardy, a certain care is helpful. There are many names given to many things, and usually it does not pay the local merchant or hotel to be well stocked in the more distinct brands. If you want to buy a bottle of wine, make sure it is not bottled locally but at the place of origin. That is to say, you should not choose in San Remo a (Piedmontese) *Barbera* that carries a trade mark from anywhere but a place in Piedmont. You may have to pay a little more if you insist on having the right thing from the right place—but you will receive incomparably better value!

The explanation is very simple. With a few exceptions, *château* or estate bottling as we know it in France does not exist in Italy. Firstly, the *châteaux* have developed into wine companies who do their trading. Secondly, the merchants do their own growing, and in addition also buy the harvest of independent farmers whose cultivation they control and supervise under long-standing contracts.

In the good years, the shippers keep the entire harvest for maturing and subsequent bottling under their trade marks, though they may sell a small proportion in casks to trusted customers in the catering business. They are keen on keeping up their reputation. To ship their top produce to other places in casks instead of only in bottles, would enable another merchant to bottle it and pass it off as his own produce.

What they do sell in quantity, not bottled but in barrels, is the wine that has not quite come up to expectation. The outside trader who buys it (in districts with no sizeable wine-production he must do so) is of course perfectly within his right to name this wine, which now comes under his trade mark, according to the type and place of origin. However, if the seat of the firm as stated on the label, and the region of growth as indicated by the type, do not correspond, there is always the possibility that the quality of the wine is not quite what it could, and should, be!

The loving care of the local people for their local wine

over many centuries has produced an infinite variety of excellent wines all over Italy. Some of them have become internationally known, others have not. Very often the sole reason for a wine being known lies in the fact that it is available in manageable quantity. I used to visit a friend of mine at Faenza who always offered me a fantastic red wine called *Savignon*. He buys it from the tenant of a big landowner near Forlì, who is the only one among the many tenants of the estate to cultivate it in one particular vineyard on one particular slope of one particular hill. The vine is said to have been imported during a period of French occupation in the time of Napoleon, and did not produce appreciable results on any other site, so that its cultivation elsewhere was abandoned. To-day this one tenant prides himself that not even the owner of the estate has ever tasted it. He keeps it for himself and sells an occasional demijohn to my friend. Such is wine. Such are the lovers of wine.

Some rather good *Savignon* is also produced in the district of Gorizia, near Trieste, also dating back to Napoleonic days. I do not think it is available over here, but if you come across it at some place in Northern Italy you would do well to try it. It is not an extraordinary wine, such as "my" private *Savignon*, but it is worth drinking for a change. Not all vintages are equal; the best should have a faint metallic tinge superimposed over the strong, fiery taste.

The variety of Italian wines is probably much wider than that of any other country, even France, where large districts know no viticulture at all. Although Italy is a much smaller producer than France, in total output, you see the first vines already fairly high up in the mountains as soon as you have crossed the Mt. Cenis or Simplon or St. Bernard passes. From there down the steep valleys, over hilly country, through the plains, up again in the Appenines, along both coast lines to the southernmost tip of Sicily, there is hardly a spot where vineyards are completely absent. Some are perhaps nothing more than a few strings of vines flung across the forecourt of the modest home of the signal man along the railway line; others are endless rows of high staked vines in the even fields of the Po plain, or crowded hills covered with the bulging growth of grapes stretching in the distance farther than the eye can see, or gracious garlands winding up and down between mulberry trees for miles on end.

The incessant heat makes the grapes ripe even in higher altitudes, the riches of the soil and the strong diffusion of light allow the planting of vines interspersed among other more essential crops. There is boundless variation in the methods used in training the vines. Often the mode of training is not so much intended for the benefit of the growing grapes, as for the sake of the corn and fruit trees which have to grow on the same ground. Yet each of those varying modes naturally influences the formation of the grape, its vinosity, its acidity, and its sugar potential.

The grape seems to be a sort of chameleon among the berries. Other berries thrive or perish according to whether or not they find the proper conditions for their growth. The grape—so long as one does not expose it to outrageous climatic conditions—changes instantly. It may change its looks, it does change its appearance to the palate, as soon as it has to undergo a change of environment. The varying soil conditions, rocky, stony, sandy, loamy, chalky, clayey, alter its growth. The innumerable mineral substances contained in the soil, ferreous, sulphuric and others, not only influence its taste, but also its later behaviour when pressed into juice and left to ferment. The angle under which the sun beats onto the vineyard, the amount of heat reflected from the ground, everything and anything has a definite bearing on what will later be wine. What is best for one variety may not be at all good for another. Moreover, these three main factors—formation of terrain, soil composition, and climatic differences—bring forth an infinite number of combinations in their mingled influence on the characteristics of the grape. With the Italian peninsula plus Sicily stretching over a distance of some 700 miles, the various Italian wines grow under considerably different climatic conditions, and the geological circumstances are equally wide apart.

Generally speaking, the various districts plant different sorts of vines according to the varying conditions the vine has to meet. But many a grape harvested, say, somewhere around Naples, and the wine made of it, originally derives from the same stem as one grown in Piedmont under a different name; yet the two variations of the same breed have developed so differently that to all practical purposes they have nothing whatever in common.

It would be fascinating, but is of course quite impossible, to follow up all these strands; but then, on the way from the wine glass to the pages of this book much of the charm would be lost. Very seldom one could say that one of these vines has degenerated in the course of its migration. Usually the two or three varieties compare well with each other, although their characteristics no longer betray their common origin.

To return to a point from the previous pages, while in Italy it is hardly good policy to choose a wine from a different district, with the exception of *Chianti*, which goes all round the country, there is not much interchange between the various provinces of Italy. Each of them produces such excellent qualities that there is no need to ship the wines from one place to the other. This trend is so strong that many, even some of the best, Italian wines are hardly known outside their own districts. I think there is a better selection of Piedmontese wines in London than you will find in Verona, and it would be almost hopeless to ask in Florence for a wine grown in the Verona district! Moreover, you would deeply offend the wine-waiter who is certainly a local man. In consequence, on a journey through Italy your taste will undergo many changes, which is one of the pleasures of travelling in Italy.

There are some types of wine you are sure to miss when moving about a lot. There is no equivalent anywhere in Italy, for instance, to the excellent and well-known *Soave di Verona;* but then, you do not find the trout from the Lake of Garda, which are so delicious with it, anywhere else either. In fact, the food varies as much from place to place as the wine does. In the Romagna, for one thing, the foremost dish is poultry, and quite rightly the favourite white wine has a certain fringe of sweetness. Or if you have been longing for the incomparable black *Barolo* ever since you left Turin, as I always do, do not forget that where you are now the "filet de boeuf" to go with it will not be available either, at least not in the same sublime quality. I sometimes wonder whether the Italians cultivate their wines to enhance their food or whether it works the other way round?

II

Outside Italy the word "Chianti" has become nearly synonymous for "Italian wine".

There is a lot to be said for *Chianti*. Among other things, the production in the Chianti district is the best organized among the various vine-growing zones of Italy. With some fairly slight variations, which bring about a pleasant if superficial variety between the different brands of *Chianti*, the growers and merchants (they are mostly both at the same time) have succeeded in maintaining from one year to the other a very high and uniform standard of their produce, with hardly perceptible changes between very good and not quite so good vintage years. The processing is very skilfully carried out. The growers are excellent planners. Also, in their design to produce a standard quality they are helped by the fact that the zone of Chianti is by far the widest wine-growing district in Italy with identical (or nearly identical) conditions of soil, terrain, and climate. Every other Italian wine is either very limited in quantity; or, if it is the vine and not the locality which gives its name to the wine, it varies from place to place to such a degree as to defy common denomination. This certainly impairs the marketability of a great number of the other Italian wines.

However, I believe that much, if not most, of the popularity of *Chianti* has to do with the really pretty wicker flasks in which the wine comes. These caught the eye of the international public, and in consequence *Chianti* became a best seller in the international markets. I see *Chianti* flasks used as a decoration in London bars and night clubs who do not even serve the wine, just because they look so gay and inviting.

The public has come to associate a certain taste with the sight of those lovely wicker flasks, and many take this particular taste as typical of Italian wines in general. A good deal of the preference given to French wines has to do with this one-sided notion. It narrows down the Italian wines to just one item in the range of choice. *Chianti,* good, easy, and eminently drinkable as it is, cannot possibly be the right companion for everyone and everything. I am not concerned with the damage the other Italian vine-growing regions have to suffer from the exclusive *Chianti* taste of the international public; but I do feel a lot may be lost by those who think of the many Italian wines as just some other varieties of *Chianti.* More often than not they are worlds apart!

For some time now, the *Chianti* growers have established among themselves a ruling as to what may be rightly called *Chianti*: namely, the wine grown in a certain district south of Florence, a wine composed of three different sorts of grapes. The *zona classica di Chianti,* extending between Florence and Siena, is fairly small, only about 61,000 hectar—that is, just over 150,000 acres. For this wine the growers established a seal, a black cockerel on a golden background, which goes on every flask in addition to the individual trade label. Nobody else is allowed to use it.

However, very soon the *zona classica* had to concede that the surrounding districts of Tuscany—producing wine which is in no definable way different from or inferior to the hard core *Chianti* (the "Chianti classico") —also had every right to call their wine *Chianti.* For this *Chianti* another seal was established, a white *putto* designed after the many Della Robbia angels you see all over Florence. It testifies that the flask bearing it contains a wine which, although it is not grown in the inner zone of Chianti, has all the characteristics typical of it. A wonderful system by which the customer can be perfectly sure of what he buys. For there had been wine-merchants who cashed in on the immense popularity of *Chianti* at home and abroad, and produced something more or less —mostly less—similar to it, and could call it *Chianti* without hindrance. They can still do so, of course— because the word "Chianti" is not legally protected as for instance the word "Cognac" is, but they cannot get the seal applied to their product.

It is a curious fact that one of the foremost *Chianti* growers, Ricasoli, uses the name *Chianti* only for the younger vintages bottled in wicker flasks. His superior table wines, of older and exquisite vintage, come in ordinary bottles under the names of his two castles, Brolio and Meleto, which top the hills of his vineyards. Indeed, there are not many red wines anywhere on earth which could be better than these select vintage *Chiantis*. The one does not bear the word "Chianti" anywhere on the label, the other carries it only in very small print, as though it were of no real importance. In the mid fifties I found a bottle of *Brolio* 1923 at the restaurant Canelli in Turin which was a sheer delight. And, at the same place, I had a 1937 *Meleto*, equally good, with a distinct shade of onion skin in its colour, which is by no means characteristic for *Chianti* in general. In either case, I could not imagine that anybody would realize without having studied the label that the bottle came from the Chianti district.

Several other growers, too, follow a similar practice in order to distinguish their top qualities from the rest. The trouble, in this case, as with many other Italian high vintage qualities, is that the wines are little known; consequently, failing the customers' request for them, they are rarely obtainable outside Italy.

It may not, perhaps, be widely known that *Chianti* is not as straight a produce as wines normally are. Three sorts of grapes go to make it. Red "San Giovese" grapes, in the first place, and a good proportion of white "Trebbiano" and "Malvasia" are processed together. And you will notice a certain sparkle, *un frizzantino* as the Italians say, more the feel of a prickle on the tongue than a definite effervescence. The younger the *Chianti*, the more pronounced this is. It comes from a very small, strongly-coloured red grape added after the fermentation has come to an end, which causes a second fermentation, so-called *govano*. Light though it is, it persists for a long while even after the wine has been cleared and bottled, and subsides completely only in the older vintages. I rather like it; it adds to the refreshing quality of the *Chianti* wines. One will find a similar "frizzantino" also in some other Italian wines, though with them it originates from a different cause.

"White Chianti", which one sees very frequently, is really a misnomer. Strictly speaking, only the composite product of those grapes is *Chianti,* and indeed the seals I mentioned before are only applied to this one. However, the white wines of the zone, those made from the grapes which otherwise go into the *Chianti* together with the red grapes, are none the worse when they stand on their own. I remember one of them, called *Arbia* after the river in the valley where it is grown, as being really excellent.

Boswell, I read in his "Grand Tour", among many other experiences had one with a near relative of *Chianti*. In Siena, he writes: "I regaled myself with delicious

Montepulciano". *Montepulciano* still exists, coming from a small place South of Siena, and is sometimes to be seen in shops in London and New York. Bottled abroad, it may not be absolutely the best thing one can obtain in this line, but considering its exceptionally cheap price it is good value for your money.

Vin Nobile di Montepulciano is indeed a very good wine—light bodied, fresh as the air of the green hills of Tuscany, of the same strength (11 to 13 per cent alcoholic content—19 to 23° proof spirit) as *Chianti*, a little darker in colour, with some superior vintages to its credit.

Brunello di Montalcino is another Tuscany wine one frequently meets when travelling there, very much the same as the *Vin Nobile*. I always wonder, when I come upon these places, why one never takes a holiday in Tuscany proper? We stick to the noble towns of Florence and Siena, rush through the lovely landscape on our way to Rome, but we never pause for a rest in this panoramic smile of grey olives, green vines and black cypresses with gracious villas nestling on the hill-tops.

Have you ever seen San Gimignano with its slender towers shooting out from a cluster of steep houses perched together on a pointed little mountain? A very good light white wine comes from there, *Vernaccia*. It has little pretences but a fresh, dry taste and a harmonious, slightly bitter bouquet. Together with the pale, tender *Montecarlo* it stands as typical of the white variety among the otherwise predominantly red wines of Tuscany.

III

One of the finest wine-growing districts of Italy is that of Verona, with the hills to the North of the town stretching eastwards from the Lake of Garda. Soft valleys lie sunning themselves between the gentle hills which rise towards the high mountains that protect the vineyards from the cold winds of the North.

Although we automatically associate Verona with the image of Juliet and Romeo, I find the town still essentially Roman in character, much more so than any other place in Italy—Rome included! Is it only because of the Roman Arena dominating the centre, and the charming Roman Theatre built into the steep rock on the other side of the river? All the palazzi and churches are, of course, medieval or renaissance, but I could easily imagine the people of Verona walking about in togas without changing their habits to any extent.

The viticulture of the region dates back even much farther than Roman days. The Etruscans, known for their skill at vine-growing, had settled here far back in history, before they were driven up the Adige valley. Evidence of primitive wine-making was found in excavations of bronze age lake-dwellings on the shores of Lake Garda.

Soave is an ancient village clustered around a hill a few miles east of Verona. It gave its name to the white wine grown around it, and "suave" indeed the wine is. *Soave* has a soft, velvety taste, with a faint recollection of sweetness; it is so clear and dry that nothing of its subtle bouquet is ever lost. It is not a wine which need mature for a great length of time. I cannot imagine anything that can be added to the perfection of a great vintage, which is generally at its best after five to seven years. It tastes as a very clear, sunny sky might taste if one could drink it! An indefinable something which one can hardly describe as a sparkle gives a pleasant individuality to its gay character. This is explained by the volcanic background of the terrain which causes a certain slowing down in the process of fermentation so that infinitesimal traces remain for long after.

All wines here are fairly light, with an alcohol content of around 11% (equivalent to 19 plus degrees proof spirit), perhaps a little less than the strength of *Chianti*. It makes them a particularly pleasant drink in summer, when one should beware of wines that go easily to the head. Yet after a visit to the cellars and vineyards of one of the two principal grower-shippers of Verona, I must admit I welcomed the kind suggestion to indulge in a little *siesta* at the very unconventional hour of 5 o'clock. Probably I had been too thorough. Whenever I see wine, and whenever I arrive in Italy for that matter, I melt like chocolate in a baby's hand. My two hosts on that occasion, Conte Rizzardi and Signor Tiboni, had been more careful than I was, as they did not empty any of their dozen or so glasses. But then they had to drive the cars.

It was a great occasion, and a wonderful experience, which I shall always be glad to remember. These huge oak casks in the dimly lit cellars have something monumental about them, in age as well as in size. Those holding 50 and 100 hectolitres, that is up to 2,000 gallons, are by no means the biggest: if you are a lady and figures mean nothing to you, let me say that some of these barrels are about the size of a large furniture van. Concrete cisterns have been introduced in recent years;

they are of course much easier to empty and to clean. But for maturing and aging the wine needs oak around it. Therefore the producers have arrived at a compromise between old custom and technical progress. They use the cisterns only for the young wine in its first stages of fermentation. During that time it is transferred from one cistern to the other at intervals so that the deposit which comes to rest at the bottom is gradually left behind. The process is repeated until the wine becomes step by step crystal clear and ready to be transferred into oak.

The three most renowned red wines of Verona are the *Valpolicella*, the *Valpantena*, and the *Bardolino*. They are all emphatically southern in character, bright, ruby red, very dry, lively and fresh. The three are virtually the same thing, coming from the same vines, and only the difference of sites accounts for slight variations between one and the other. Valpolicella and Valpantena are two valleys running up from the plain through the hills, Bardolino is a village on the eastern shore of the Lake of Garda, opposite the thin silver-green peninsula of Sirmione. The bouquet of the *Valpantena* somehow reminds me of the austere scent of the last autumn leaves still on the trees, and the *Bardolino* brings the perfumed memory of raspberries to my mind.

All of them are excellent from their first year on, with the *Valpolicella* aging best of all. I remember one of 1938 vintage which would have nothing to fear from comparisons with the finest *Clarets*. *Bardolino*, I should say, is at its best in its fifth or sixth year, and is not likely to improve further.

The comparatively high quality of Italian wines while they are still young, is in my opinion one of their most pleasing features. I like the spontaneous freshness of the young wine before it has achieved perfect roundness.

Old vintage wines every day can be almost too much of a good thing.

This may sound very snobbish and superior, but somehow it brings to my mind the old story of *toujours perdrix*. Risking a disdainful yawn from my older readers, I shall relate it for the sake of the younger ones, who, I suspect, may have never heard of it.

In the time of the reign of Louis XV., there was a French marquis who was strongly reproved by his priest because—alas!—he was unfaithful to his young, beautiful and charming marquise. "Let us speak about it again in three weeks' time", said the marquis. "And tell me, Monsieur l'Abbé, what is your favourite meal?"

This question deflated the good Father's zeal, and he confessed to having a great weakness for partridges. For the next week the priest received his favourite partridges at every meal, and enjoyed them to the full. During the second week he left some of the game on his plate, and during the third, looked with a certain amount of envy at the roast meat, fish and fowl to which his hosts served themselves.

"You don't look very happy, Father", observed the marquis just before the end of the third week. "Tell me, what is the reason?"—"It is always partridges", sighed the priest, *"toujours perdrix"*.

I shall never forget a cellar party (or was it an inspection?) at Monteforte d'Alpone, on the top-gallery of the two-storey high cisterns of *Soave*. It was early in summer and the wine we drank only from the last harvest. The fermentation was just over, but the wine still started "boiling" when the valves, or lids, of the enormous concrete containers were opened as we dipped our glasses into the bright golden liquid to sample it. It is true that normally one does not get wine which promises to be one of extra quality, while it is still young. The growers naturally intend to obtain the best value for their produce, and do not sell it. But generally speaking, in Italy even those wines which are not allowed to mature but are sold "open" when still quite young, are much better than in other wine-producing countries. I think this has to do with the lower acidity of Italian wines (0·40 to 0·50 "fixed" acid against 0·80 to 0·90 in the French ones).

The same element seems also to account for another characteristic of the Italian wines: their distinct fruity flavour. I do not mean the occasional sensation of strawberry and other fruit in some varieties. In general the wines preserve a distinct idea of fresh grapes in their bouquet which is the more pronounced the younger they are. I think this is one of the most attractive qualities of the wines of Italy.

Mostly from the eastern shores of Lake Garda, comes a *vin rosé*, which is much stronger than the French type and equal in strength to the other Veronese wines: *Chiaretto del Garda*. It is made of red grapes treated *a modo bianco*—"the white way". The husks of white grapes are immediately removed in the process of pressing, because they contain too high a proportion of (bitter) tannic acid. With red grapes, in contrast, the husks are allowed to soak in the juice for some time, in order to impart as much of their colour as possible. If the husks are taken away immediately an in-between product is obtained, a very pale red wine of light body, the *Chiaretto*. I think the growers produce it mostly for curiosity's sake, to create a very agreeable variation.

Bertani's have now adopted a specially designed oval-shaped flask for it, wicker-covered like the *Chianti* flasks, to set the type apart from their other wines. *Chiaretto* should be served slightly cooled; not so much as white wines, but room temperature as applied to other red wines is certainly not suitable for it. It goes with any dish which does not definitely require either red or white wine. It is most pleasant with chicken and veal, and goes well with the Italian *pasta asciutta*. A considerable quantity of *Chiaretto del Garda* is exported to the United States, but to meet the American taste this is produced in a semi-sweet quality, instead of its usual dry one.

A traditional speciality of the region is the famous Veronese *Recioto*. It is something quite exceptional, a full bodied red sparkling wine made of *uva passita*— dried grapes. The name *Recioto* derives from a dialectical expression for the Italian *orecchio*—ear. It is descriptive of the process applied to the harvesting of the grape: the lower middle part of each bunch of grapes is cut off before full ripening, and only the two upper clusters at its sides—the "ears" as it were—are left on the stem and allowed to develop to complete ripeness. After harvesting, the trunkated bunches of grapes are placed (under cover, of course) on large racks made of reed-canes and left to dry well into January. Then they are pressed, but instead of receiving the usual *passito* treatment, whereby a highly alcoholic and very sweet wine is obtained (I shall speak of it later), the young *Recioto* is processed in the same way as *champagne*.

The result is indeed unique. It is not *champagne*. It is a dense, deep red, rich sparkling wine, demi-sec— what the Italians call *amabile* with 12—13% alcoholic content (21—23 proof). When only one year old a fairly strong aroma of raspberry is perceptible which slowly fades as the wine becomes more balanced with age.

I should not call it a dessert wine, but a wine to be drunk by itself. Unfortunately, not very much of it is available. It is produced from Valpolicella and Valpantena grapes grown on one particular hill and on a few neighbouring sites, with a total yield of 7,000 hectolitres, equivalent to 150,000 gallons or under one million bottles—in the good years.

Farther east from Verona, Soave, Valpantena and Valpolicella, as the mountains that stretch towards the Austrian border flatten our over hilly land into the plain, a good many wines are produced which are reasonably comparable to those three top qualities. Most of the red wines are sold under the name of *Vino Veronese;* the white ones are usually called *Trebbiano,* after the vine which is also the basis of the nobler *Soave.*

This is a good example of how an apparently slight variation in climatic conditions can bring about a considerable difference in quality. Here the defile of the hills is lined up, roughly speaking, from South-West to North-East, so that it is open towards the East and exposed to the currents of cold air. Soave and the other vine-growing places of Verona proper are so sheltered between the hill-sides running from North to South, that they are shielded against any harsh influence. One might not notice much difference in climate oneself, but the grapes, more sensitive than we are, do!

Gambellara, Vicenza, Treviso, Conegliano are the best known centres of production. Their biggest outlet is Venice and the smaller holiday places and lidos near Venice, where there is no viniculture of its own standing. The straw-coloured *Colli Euganei* and *Garganega* and the light golden *Colli Trevigliani* are names to keep in mind. With your diet in all the osterias, trattorias and

Kuechelberger (the name comes from the hill at the foot of the Castel Tirolo where it grows) is the house-wine of Merano.

Silvaner (white) comes from Brixen; its cultivation on some sites goes up to 2,600 feet.

A speciality of the South-Tyrolian wines is the white *Gewuerztraminer*. "Gewuerz" is German for "spices": that does not mean that spices are added to *Traminer* wine, but that for reasons unknown its aroma is so strong that the word is hardly sufficient to convey the idea of its strength. It is quite an experience to have this wine with hors d'oeuvres.

The red *Kalterer* (from the Lago Caldaro near Bolzano) is very popular all over South Tyrol, probably because it is somewhat lighter than most of the other wines; it is a very lively wine, but tends to be a little rough at times. *Lagarino*, from the Bolzano hills, is also in the lighter red category, not a high class wine perhaps, but pleasant enough to drink. Its aroma is puzzling. Some people insist that it has a touch of vanilla. I am quite prepared to admit this—certainly there is something difficult to define about it.

So much for the dry wines, with an apology to the many I have been unable to account for. Even my resistence to the incessant delights of glittering wines has a limit, and to make things worse I can never make up my mind whether to indulge in pleasures already experienced, or to venture into new ones.

It is always an awe-inspiring ceremony, when the host, after opening a new bottle, lines up a row of crystal-clear glasses for his guests, pours a few drops in the first one, swings it round, pours the wine over to the next, swings it round, and so on to the last glass from which he flings it away with a light hand. But what does he really exorcise? Only the illusion that some faintly perfumed trace of an alien wine may have clung to the glass. The impressive ceremonial in no way prevents us from becoming light-headed, though one wishes it could.

Lovers of *Moscato,* which is usually connected with more southern regions, will find this sweet delight nearly everywhere here in a quality distinctly apart from other *Moscato* growths. The Alto Adige *Moscato,* limpid and fresh, is not quite as sweet and dense as *Moscato* usually is, and makes up for it with a much higher alcohol content.

I cherish happy memories of Castel Ranuncolo—Burg Runkelstein in the Talfer valley not far from Bolzano. One afternoon in May, two friends and I had come there after a little walk and dropped in for tea and something to eat. There was plenty to eat, but there was no tea, there was *Moscato.* With this golden-yellow liquid "high tea" became sheer poetry. As we sat at one of the deep windows, cut into the thick walls, looking out high over the dream-like beauty of the valley, we became more and more dreamy ourselves and were no longer sure whether the white clouds really floated in the blue sky over our heads . . . they seemed to stray into our legs. The limpid blue turned softly into the star-studded canopy of night. Walking home was no longer a practical suggestion, and we were faced with the alternative of summoning a taxi from Bolzano to take us back to the hotel, or to stay overnight where we were. We stayed.

There is no great difference between the many other *Moscato* wines of Italy. The aroma is bound to be basically the same specific Muscat one, and Moscatello grapes are grown nearly everywhere in Italy. A great deal are marketed as grapes, while a good proportion of what is pressed goes into the production of Vermouth and Brandy, and only a comparatively small quantity of the best growths come out as *Moscato* wine.

Conditions of environment do not seem to add more than marginal variations to its flavour. What makes the Alto Adige *Moscato* (frequently called *Moscato Atesino*) so particularly attractive to me is, as I said, its freshness and light body, and certainly its high alcohol content of 13 to 15 per cent (23 to 26 proof), for this allows it to carry 6 to 10 per cent sugar and yet remain a proper wine.

As a good second of my *Moscato* preferences, I should give the Piedmontese *Moscato d'Asti*. Its character is very similar to that of the *Atesino,* but it is much less alcoholic, only 7 to 10% (about 12 to 17° proof). Rather an advantage on occasions! The sugar content of the *Moscato* wines of Asti varies strongly from 5 to 12 per cent, as every grower in the district has his own system of making his wine. Some use fresh grapes, others take dried *(passito)* grapes in various stages of dryness, some prefer grapes which were left on the vines as long as weather permitted so that they come to dry slightly while still on the stems.

It is quite impossible to follow up all these varieties in detail, admirable as they are in showing the growers' loving understanding for their grapes and their skill in producing from each grape the best wine it is able to yield. Probably, the one with the best counts to its credit is Gancia's *Moscato Passito d'Asti,* very delicate and clear, much lighter and not so dense as the *Moscato Passito* wines of the Italian South. Also, it ages extremely well and may come very near to the standard of what is called *Vin Santo.*

There is a fair supply of it available in most places in Italy as well as abroad. The greatest part, however, of the *Moscato* harvest of Asti is reserved for the enormous *Spumante* production of the district.

If you go farther South, I should like you to remember *Moscatello di Montalcino* (Tuscany), with not much alcohol (9 to 10%—16 to 17° proof), and also an exceptionally low sugar content (only 4 to 5 per cent), which makes it a very refreshing drink.

Moscato di Terracina (Latium, the province of Rome) is in roughly the same range. It is a wine to think of in connection with the glorious Roman pastries and gateaux with whipped cream and candied fruit. I shall not tempt you to imitate the dizzier side of my own experiences, but if one tea time you feel like eating lots and lots of sweet things, do not ask for tea, choose *Terracina* as an accompaniment instead.

From Sardinia comes *Moscato di Tempio*, the least sweet and most alcoholic of them all: 2 to 4 per cent sugar, and 12 to 13 per cent alcohol (21 to 23° proof). Most of it is presented as sparkling wine, but whether sparkling or straight, *Tempio* is very scarce.

Farther towards the South, the *Moscato* wines are usually extremely heavy, in alcohol content as well as in sugar, and almost exclusively made of dried grapes—*uva passita*—grapes, that is, which after harvesting have been left to dry on racks for anything up to two months so that some two thirds of their liquid content may evaporate.

There is a very nice story told of a poor farmer who lived on his own on poor land which gave only very poor, sour wine. One day, just as he had harvested his grapes, a friend rushed in to ask his help in a desperate emergency. The man could not possibly refuse, left his baskets full of grapes standing were they were, and followed his friend, very worried about how he would find his grapes on his return. Naturally, he expected them to rot, and feared his supply of wine for the year would be lost. But on the contrary, when he returned after several days, the grapes, though shrivelled, were perfectly intact, and when he pressed them he got the best wine he had ever had.

This story of smiling heaven rewarding a good deed, is supposed to have happened with only the slightest of variations in Greece, in Italy, in France, and in Spain, everywhere, then, where grapes are dried for wine-making. However, the tale is not true to life, because very sour grapes do not dry well at all, nor would a few days in a basket dry even the sweetest of grapes. But somehow or other, somebody must have discovered that when the grapes were spread out on mats or racks, the dry air of the Mediterranean winter was apt to reduce their liquid content, and therefore increase the sugar proportion. In consequence, the wine then produced was stronger than normal; it could even be brought to a high degree of strength and still retain some sugar.

I believe that the main reason for drying grapes before pressing was because people wanted a sweet wine for a change, and arrived at the right system by much trial and error, before experts began to probe scientifically into the problem of how the the right effect could be obtained.

In England, we have almost entirely lost the taste for sweet wines, though I recall that Pitt is reported to have retired after dinner for a night's work in the flickering candle-light of his room in Downing Street, with maps of Europe and the world laid out on the table, and seven (the holy number!) bottles of Port. Well, to the people of the Mediterranean countries their sweet wine does not signify high politics. It means a pleasant hour while they sit with friends and relatives round the dinner table, with the satisfaction of a happy meal passed, and nibble fresh almonds and sip their golden *Moscato*. "Idling over the nuts", we would say, only that we allow ourselves this quiet pleasure only once a year—at Christmas. Why, indeed, not more often?

The strongest *Moscato* wines of the South of Italy are:
Salento,
Moscato di Lucania, and
Moscato di Trani, whose alcoholic content reaches 15 per cent (26° proof spirit), with up to 20% sugar. A much lighter type of both the Lucania and Trani varieties is produced from grapes only slightly dried.

Moscato di Cosenza (Calabria) has the same alcoholic level, but is not quite as sweet.

The best alcohol/sugar balance is probably achieved in the *Moscato di Pentelleria* (on that tiny island halfway between Sicily and Tunis) with 14% alcohol and 11% sugar. It has an extremely pleasant taste of dried grapes particular to it. However, the production is so small that the wine is almost a rarity.

Passito di Siracusa, and
Moscato di Noto come from Sicily. They are very similar to the Pentelleria quality, though more dense in body. The Muscat aroma is strongly pronounced in both. The one of Siracusa is, I think, the most widely marketed of all.

Moscato del Campidano, from Sardinia, catches the imagination with a very characteristic bouquet. It is equal in strength to the others, but with only 8 per cent sugar it is not so sweet, which is rather to its advantage. Alas! not much of it is available.

V

In a Hollywood film "Ulysses" there is a scene in which the Greeks who had been captured by the Giant Polyphemos offer him some of the wine they carry. Enthusiastically the Giant asks for more. Whereupon the Greeks ask him to gather a load of grapes from the slope of the hill outside his hideous cave, which they then press, and let him drink the liquid. Instantaneously intoxicated, as we should say in legal language, the Giant falls conveniently asleep, and the Greeks manage to escape. I wonder whether Homer, the Greek bard of some 3,000 years ago who is supposed to have composed the original version of the saga now made into a film, imagined the process of wine-production to be as simple as that! However, it appears so in the modern screen version of the old "Odyssey".

Vine-growers all over the world would be only too glad if there were nothing more to do but to press grapes in order to produce wine. In fact, the fresh juice pressed from the grapes contains as much alcohol as any other fruit juice—none at all. It is only by a long process, liable to many mischances, that at some stage on its way from the pleasantly tasting grapes to the goblet of the enchanted drinker the grape juice develops alcohol, and WINE is born.

The original liquid is just "must". By the way, if you ever happen to be in a vine-growing district between the end of September and the beginning of November, ask for it. "Must" is a very pleasant drink, sweet, smooth, slightly cloudy, non-alcoholic of course. I always try to

39

have some if I can do so during the few weeks when it is available.

The "must" from every pressing of grapes keeps only for a very short time, perhaps a day or two, as sweet and fresh as the grapes taste. Then it becomes "stormy" as the growers say: the fermentation by which the sugar content of the grape juice is transformed into alcohol has set in. The "must" is quite undrinkable during that time—opaque, turbid, and with an unpleasant, sour taste. You will notice the process of fermentation going on as soon as you come near a grower's cellar in harvest time: the noise of the new wine fermenting in the barrels sounds like the waves of the sea, like the noise you hear when you put a large sea-shell next to your ear . . . *il vino bolle,* say the Italians—the wine is "boiling".

On the Sicilian coast beneath Mt. Etna they still show you the four boulders the blinded Giant is supposed to have hurled at the ship of the escaping Greeks. They are still there for you to see. The wine is there also, the so-called *Etna,* probably the most widely distributed of the good Sicilian table wines. There is both white *Etna* and red for the tables of Sicily; the white possesses about 12% of alcoholic content; the red *Etna* in its older vintages reaches easily 14% (21° and 24° proof spirit respectively). I think the deep garnet coloured *Etna* is the better of the two; it ages very well. The white one, very pale, with a pleasant-to-look-at greenish tinge to its straw colour, is very refreshing in the hot climate of this beautiful island.

I love thinking of Sicily almost more than being there. If one arrives at Palermo from Milan, Genoa, and Rome with their glass-plated modern buildings—all chromium, super-American, symbols of the fight for achievement— the old-fashioned Sicilian capital, heavy with the weight of by-gone greatness, comes almost as a shock. Does the

arrogance of these *palazzi* defy the misery of the poor?
Yet, for many decades, a great deal of the cavalier
attitude of the leading class had its roots in a grinding
resentment against Sicily's inclusion into the unified
Italian State. Now, since Sicily was given a form of
autonomous status a few decades ago, things have
started to move there also; they may move slowly, but
this slowness bears the stamp of solidity.

What remains with me, in retrospect, is an image of
patriarchal calm. I see the father of some Sicilian friends
of mine, an old, silver-haired gentleman dressed in a
well-cut shantung suit, bent over huge baskets of figs,
oranges, and grapes which the servants have brought up
to the dining room. With great care he selects the best
fruits one by one for the dinner table of the family. Are
they so rich? Hardly. They belong to nothing more than
to what we should call upper middle class. But fruit and
oil and wheat and everything we need to have shipped at
great expense from God knows where, they grow for
themselves on their own doorstep.

The son is a lawyer: that means, he studied law in
order to be able to put an impressive brass plate on the
door of the house, and also, I suspect, to have an excuse
for spending some years of his youth away from home in
the big cities! Now he supervises the work on the land
which has come to him through generations. He sees to
it that new trees are planted in time to replace the old
ones; he talks with his tenants about what and when and
where to plant; he sends a builder when their houses
need repair . . . in other words, he walks over his fields
early in the morning and later in the afternoon—not
more exacting physically than playing a round of golf.

Is it work? Nobody of the landed class in Sicily does
much more; and except, of course, the poor—who are

indeed very poor—there are not many people there who have not some land to their names. They adjust their lives to the size of the land they have inherited. None of them will ever have much cash in their bank accounts, not even the richer ones; but then, their way of life does not involve so much spending as ours. Last, but not least, they have the sun as a source of contentment which never pales.

Nor are they obliged to pay any sort of exorbitant duty before they can enjoy a bottle of wine. They leave that to us, backward as they are . . . as they also leave it to us to work seven hours a day in the City in order to organize the production and transportation and distribution of every egg until it costs four times as much as it would if we could decide to leave the job to the hens and to a little woman who brings the new-laid eggs every day to the kitchen in a little basket.

It was at Catania that I heard for the first and only time in my life of "dog catcher wine".

"Father", said my friend Faustina, "could you please fill up a bottle of the dog catcher wine?"

What did she mean? Faustina has two setters, of very noble English breed, who love a walk on their own. Whenever the two are not in at meal times, the family know the dogs have been caught by the dog catcher. Though he knows the setters perfectly well and could leave them to find their own way home, his duty is to see that there are no stray dogs about the place. It is not his business to decide which dog is a "stray" in the true sense of the word and which one merely strolls about for pleasure. And if he let the two setters roam as they please, Faustina would not come and retrieve them for the statutory charge of 100 lire, plus 200 lire tip and a bottle of wine. It is his contribution towards social equality, and the two English setters well see to it that his income is thus augmented at least once a week. Broadly speaking, dry, or even nearly dry, good table wines are almost a rarity in Sicily, as well as over the whole South of Italy. The sun is over-generous down there. Neither the rich sugar content it produces in the grapes, nor their rapid growth and ripening make for a delicate bouquet, and the strongly volcanic terrain often taints the juice with a certain after-taste which is not very pleasing to the tongue. This after-taste fades away with the years, but only very few of the wines of the extreme South are fit for even average aging.

There are, however, some places where these influences are either not so strong as they are in most vineyards, or are balanced by more favourable ones. These exceptions are really excellent, and what persists as a constant feature of all Southern Italian wines is their extremely high alcoholic content. However, as far as I know, they are rarely shipped abroad. I think it best to put down here a fairly comprehensive list of all those varieties one should look for when on the spot:

Mamertino, white, dry, comes from the Messina district. Ages very well. Its alcoholic content goes up to 15% (26° proof), which is already rather exceptional for a white wine. Very aromatic bouquet with a nicely perceptible sweet background going well with the golden yellow colour.

The red *Eloro,* dry, also from Sicily, is of equal alcoholic degree. I like the bright garnet glitter.

Faro, red, dry, grows on the hills overlooking the straights of Messina; it is of very good everyday quality, rich in taste, of medium strength (12%—21° proof, or slightly more). Should not be too old.

Savuto,

Cirò, and

Lacrima Castrovillari, all grow between Cosenza and Catanzaro in Calabria on the southernmost stretch of the Italian peninsula. They are good, dry, red wines. The *Savuto* should not be drunk before it is two or even three years of age; some of the older vintages are really superior wines with up to 15% (26° proof) alcohol content. The *Cirò* is somewhat lighter and does not need long to bring out its full quality of clean, genuine taste. *Lacrima* (no relative of the famous Neapolitan *Lacrima Christi*) is the lightest of the three, about 13%—23° proof, a fresh wine, already pleasing in its early years.

The mountainous region East of Naples and farther down East to the Adriatic Sea, presents us with two agreeable white table wines of medium strength (about 12%—21°):

San Severo, and

Martina Franca, dry, and pleasant, after they have properly settled down with a year or two to their credit.

There is a red wine, *Castel del Monte,* grown not far from Bari, of the same strength, dry, deep ruby in colour, with an amiable fruity bouquet which might be recognized among many. And on the slopes of the 4,300 feet high Mt. Vulture, roughly in the centre of the Lucania district, there grows the proud, deep red

Aglianico, much stronger than the former. *Aglianico del Vulture* is an excellent wine at any age, intensifying its full bouquet with every year it is allowed to rest.

The bright red *Santo Stefano,*

and the deep yellow *Torre Giulia* are two more from the Apulian region which deserve mentioning.

Vernaccia,

Nuragus,

Malvasia, and

Vermentino are the white table wines the stern granite island of Sardinia has to offer from its barren hills;

Oliena, also Sardinian, is a not too dark red wine, of quite exceptional quality, with a not unpleasant after-taste reminiscent of bitter herbs. I think it is the heaviest dry, red wine I have come across in Italy, its alcoholic content in the very good vintages approaching 16%—28° proof.

The golden *Malvasia* "di Bosa" is in the same region of strength, with a superb bouquet and slightly nutty flavour, much heavier and also to my taste better than the original *Malvasia* "di Grottaferrata", near Rome.

The *Vernaccia* "di Sardegna" with its bright amber colour is even heavier than these two, going up to 18% —31° proof spirit. Very strongly flavoured, it is fairly mellow in spite of a certain bitter tang which I find rather intriguing.

The *Vermentino* "di Gallura" is already much lighter, very delicate in flavour, and the straw coloured *Nuragus* is the lightest of them all. The latter two are those most popular in Sardinia, brought out already when they are still fairly young, whilst *Vernaccia* and *Oliena* are usually kept for good aging. Some particular *Malvasia* vintages are never offered as table wines; although dry, they are served with the dessert, and quite rightly so.

However much I appreciate those I have mentioned so far, the real distinction of Southern Italy lies in the enormous range of sweet dessert wines. When I say dessert wine, though, I do not necessarily mean a wine to be served with the fruit and sweet course. For that purpose I prefer either sparkling wines or *Moscato* or what in Italian is called *abbocato*: the demi-sec, medium dry varieties of light white wines that one cannot describe as dry, but which are not really sweet either. What I am listing on the following pages are all wines not so much meant to go with delicious Italian pastries, but rather as a dessert in themselves. Considering the quantities of food consumed during an Italian meal, one is often only capable of finishing it with something as un-substantial as a glass of sweet wine.

To round off a delightful repast you may, e.g., enjoy the magnificent soft *Aleatico*, of deep ruby red, with its characteristic, strongly pronounced bouquet, whose sweetness is enhanced by a slightly bitterish background.

There are two varieties of it, strangely enough growing at a considerable distance one from the other, on the East and West coasts of Italy. *Aleatico di Portoferraio* comes from the island of Elba, *Aleatico di Puglia* from the region of Bari, Brindisi and Taranto. The latter is slightly stronger, 15% of alcohol, compared with the 14% of the other, which, contrariwise is the sweeter of the two. Apart from that, there is hardly anything to choose between them. Both are prepared from dried grapes. They are in good supply all over Italy as well as for export.

From Sardinia come, each of them, alas, in very limited quantities, the golden *Nasco*, the purple *Monica*, and the *Girò*, whose ruby colour intriguingly verges on orange. Their sweet content varies between six and twelve per cent; it is entirely up to you which one to choose according to your mood. They are of course highly alcoholic, between 26 and 31 degrees proof spirit, in other words level with Vermouth, Port, and Sherry.

When we speak of *bouquet* in connection with wine, we have the idea of its aroma being a compound of many flavours, like flowers put together in one bunch, so that we hardly think of the individual blossoms. With the

Sardinian *Nasco* at its best, flowers come distinctly to the fore. Its bouquet is orange blossoms, unmistakeably.

The amber *Greco* from Reggio Calabria, on the very toe of the Italian boot, has this same quality, although in a less pronounced way. It is fuller in taste and not quite so delicate as *Nasco*.

Another excellent dessert wine is *Frappato di Vittoria*, grown near Ragusa on the southern point of the Sicilian triangle. As to alcohol it is in the same class. Its sugar content varies strongly with the vintages, from as little as five per cent to as much at fifteen. Cherry-red in colour, one does not forget it easily.

VI

The most famous wine of Sicily, one could almost say of all Italy, is *Marsala*, though it has gone out of fashion a little, lately. It enjoys an even higher reputation abroad than in Italy itself. Indeed it was a merchant from Liverpool, a Mr. Woodhouse, who discovered *Marsala* as long ago as in 1763, and started to commercialize the local custom of its rather complicated production.

The basic component of *Marsala* is a strongly aromatic dry white wine of normal alcohol content, grown on the extremely hot and dry soil of Trapani and Marsala, a soil saturated with ferreous substances. The second *Marsala* component consists of one quarter pure brandy (i.e., distilled wine) and three quarters of *passito* wine made from slightly dried grapes. It serves the purpose of pushing up the alcohol content of the final product. And a third component goes into *Marsala*: young, unfermented "must" which is very slowly heated up (but not boiled) until it loses about 60% of its liquid so that it becomes very dense and sweet and acquires almost the colour, and a slight taste, of caramel.

After a long period of resting, the three components are blended in an average proportion of 100:6:6, and after another rest (the whole process takes about four years) *Marsala* as we know it is ready: this rich, strong wine (17%—30½° proof spirit) of dark walnut brown colour, with that indefinable dry taste upon a basis of sweetness. For a wine that is anything but straight it has a remarkable way of aging very well, becoming more and more dry as the years go by and enriching its aroma. The best old vintages are not cheap. We call it a dessert wine to-day, but Nelson who bought large quantities of it for his sailors when he was cruising in Mediterranean waters must have thought differently.

Though *Marsala* is not what the Italians call *vino pregiato*—"a wine of high esteem", it is tremendously popular all over Italy. It stands next to the *apéritif* Vermouth in nearly every cupboard, for dessert, and there is not one café or bar or restaurant which does not serve it. Its popularity is of great advantage to the travelling public, because one can ask for a single glass and the waiter will willingly open a new bottle if necessary. The really first-class straight dessert wines are not served by the glass, and unless you are in company you may hesitate to order a bottle, or even half a bottle, if you only want a glass or two.

Marsala wine, incidentally, is in a rather amusing way connected with the history of Italy. When Garibaldi landed at Marsala, in 1860, with his corps of volunteers, to attack the Neapolitan-Sicilian Kingdom from its "weak under-belly", he met—as he had rightly antici-pated—with no immediate military resistance. But con-trary to his expectations, the Sicilian population did not greet his march of liberation with flowers and jubilation. It is difficult to say if the inhabitants of Marsala were determinedly hostile to Garibaldi's revolutionary ideas, or if they were merely a little apprehensive of those thousand or so red-shirted troops streaming ashore. At any rate, Garibaldi found all the doors locked and barred to his men, except two: Woodhouses' and Ingham's *Marsala* plants were open.

Were the two Englishmen, knowing of the support Garibaldi had found in England during his stay in the old country, more enthusiastic about his plans than the Italians? Or was it just a case of wanting to see "how the cat jumped" and a determination to ignore the situation until it clarified? Nobody can tell. In any case, here the liberators found easy going hospitality . . . until a few Royal Bourbonic gun-boats arrived off-shore, and started shelling the Garibaldians and the two English plants with them. Nobody was hurt, but some wine-barrels in the yard were hit and precious wine started flowing from the broken butts.

Whereupon the owners sent word to the Commander that he was shelling British property, and protested against its violation. The officer commanding the ships thought better of his bombardment, and steered back to Palermo. The Ingham and Woodhouse plants remained unmolested. Garibaldi's troops prepared their further operations without disturbance, they marched off and fought their way victoriously through Sicily and up to Naples. One brand of *Marsala* is still called "Garibaldi".

An Italian drink based on *Marsala* is among the best any cocktail mixer could think of, and indeed it is the only cocktail of Italian origin—*Zabbaglione,* in some places also called *Zabaione.*

Zabaione is served hot or cold, according to whether it is winter or summer. The yolk of one egg is whipped with a spoonful of sugar (preferably in an electric mixer) in as much *Marsala* as the empty shell would hold, and either heated up while being whipped, or whipped in an iced container, with some crushed ice also thrown into the mixture. Iced or heated, *Zabaione* must be all foam when served. It is wonderful for elevenses: it is nourishing and a tonic at the same time, and extremely refreshing—or warming, as the case may be.

Unfortunately, you may not obtain *Zabaione* everywhere. As with everything in Italy, so much depends on local custom. *Zabaione* is most popular in Genoa and on the Ligurian Riviera, in Rome, and in Bologna, but it is almost unknown, for instance, in Milan. However, a very good substitute for it is *frappé al Marsala,* a sort of milk-shake made with wine.

Most likely, this happy *Zabaione* marriage between egg and *Marsala*—which was of course not invented by a barman but by some unknown housewife many hundreds of years ago—gave Moroni, a distiller of Milan, the idea of producing something entirely new: *Marsaluovo.* His invention dates back to 1875, and to-day "Marsala all'uovo" is very nearly as popular as *Marsala* proper.

Moroni blended (and still does so, of course, followed by some other distillers of minor importance) one litre of *Marsala* (that is, a little less than two pints) with 3½ eggs creamed in pure alcohol. *Marsaluovo* is a lovely drink, with its 20% alcohol content (35° proof spirit) somewhat stronger than pure *Marsala.* Strangely enough, the eggs are in no way noticeable as such: they merely smooth that slightly "burnt" taste particular to *Marsala* which is not to everybody's liking, and also bring its blackish-brown colour more towards that kind of black which is the distinction of some very dark red wines. *Marsaluovo* is a drink I like especially in winter, as it makes you warm. In the cold summer of 1954 which caught me unawares in Italy with nothing but very light clothing to wear, *Marsaluovo* virtually saved my life.

Marsaluovo is probably the most typical produce of the Italian liqueur industry: I cannot think of anything similar elsewhere. It seems strange that in general Italian liqueurs and brandies should long have been relegated into second place by the French ones. In all likelihood the distilling of alcohol was known in Italy before it became known in any other country.

We know that Italian monks used some sort of brandy, obviously distilled wine, as a cure for malaria as early as the Eleventh Century. At that time, distilling must have been a very rough process, producing more or less pure alcohol—probably very effective, but certainly a ghastly drink. In the course of time, to make this medical beverage more palatable to the patients, it was infused with the juice of pressed fruits and herbs, and came to be used as a remedy against all sorts of maladies.

About 1420, a doctor of Padua concocted what was probably the first known liqueur by mixing brandy with attar of roses and added honey to sweeten it. He invented this mixture merely to prepare a pleasantly tasting medicine-brandy for one of his lady-patients, the reputedly very spoiled and extremely fussy mistress of one of the town's noblemen. But in doing so he was even more successful than he had anticipated. First the gentle lady's friends developed all sorts of illnesses in order to qualify for that delicious medicine. By and by they dropped all pretences and simply asked the doctor to sell this medicine of his which they so much enjoyed drinking. Very soon the doctor's *rosolio*—"oil of roses"—as he called it, became fashionable all over Italy, with no medical purpose attached to it.

From this original *rosolio* a number of other mixtures of brandy, honey, and fruits and herbs were developed, with oranges, cherries, apricots. They were all called *rosolio*, although the use of attar declined increasingly. Every Italian court had its *rosolio* specialists. Towards the end of the Fifteenth Century the Italians were doing a brisk export trade with their *rosolios*, and when Catarina de' Medici left Florence to marry the Dauphin of France, who became King Henry II., she included in her entourage a number of *rosolio* experts as well as some Florentine cooks. The Italians insist that these Florentines taught their art to the French.

Still, neither patriotism nor history alters the fact that later on the French makers of liqueurs overtook the Italian ones. With the exception of the Italian *Maraschino*, a liqueur made of distilled "Morello" cherries, and the excellent *VOV* egg-cocktail, there is hardly an Italian liqueur to compete with the French *Cointreau*, *Bénédictine*, or *Chartreuse* for the starring roles in international favour. However, in Italy itself, the import duty on French liqueur and *Cognac* is well-nigh prohibitive. Many Italians are snobbish enough to ignore it, but this is no reason why one should emulate them when travelling in Italy. If you feel like having a glass of liqueur, have an Italian *Triple Sec*, or *Cherry Brandy*, or whatever else you relish. They may not be as refined as their French equivalents, but in my opinion the difference in price makes up for it many times over. You may even try the Italian sweet GIN. Does it sound paradoxical that gin should be sweet? After all, there is no reason why gin which is served sweetened with orange or lime juice, should not be sweetened in the distilling process.

A very attractive Italian speciality is a liqueur called *Fior d'Alpe* by one distiller, *Edelweiss*, and *Fior delle Alpi* by another. It is prepared from aromatic herbs, Juniper, Mint, Thyme, Arnica, Marjoran, and others, gathered on the pastures and in the woods of the high mountains. Inside each bottle there is a sprig of some Alpine plant around which the excess sugar of the liqueur crystallizes—very nice to look at. This *"ramoscello"* however is not their only quality. The "Flowers of the Alps" liqueurs are much stronger than most other liqueurs are. They go up to 45% of alcohol—78° of proof spirit, against the usual liqueur gradation of 55 proof and over.

If you compare Italian BRANDY with French *Cognac* very much the same has to be said as with regard to the liqueurs. I am afraid that you will praise the *Cognac* and leave the Italian product a long way behind. But when in Italy, thinking of our usual travel allowance—though perhaps one should not think of brandy and money together—and considering the extravagant price asked for French *Cognac,* I prefer the less refined but very acceptable Italian product. *Stock Medicinal,* for instance, is not merely "not bad", but in fact quite good.

Wholehearted is my praise, though, of the Italian *Grappa.* (The word has to do with *grappolo d'uva*— "bunch of grapes"). It is distilled from the pressed husks of grapes, and achieves a level of 48% alcohol—84° proof spirit, in comparision with the 70° proof of average rum.

Grappa is not much known outside Italy, even holiday-makers in Italy are unlikely to know it. But as we are in general so keen on potent drinks, I believe this is something we are quite wrong to neglect. *Grappa* may look like water, but it tastes like fire, and very pleasant fire, similar to the Russian *Vodka.* There is also a slightly aromatic variety on the market, *Grappa Ruta,* produced with an infusion of the extract of rue. Also, in appropriate doses, *Grappa* works wonders as a cure for colds.

The Italians seem fond of herbs in every way. A stand-by of every household, and of course of every bar, is the *Fernet,* an extremely bitter, strong liqueur made with gentian, Peruvian bark, aloe, rhubarb, camomile, and other herbs. It is kept for the purpose of combating tummy upsets, a very frequent inconvenience in that country of rich, sometimes even over-rich food. Indeed, the *Fernets* are considered so medical a drink that during the years of the American prohibition they alone were admitted for sale in the United States. *Fernet Branca* is probably the best brand.

The various Italian *apéritif* liqueurs are also based on bitter herbs. I do not like them neat, as many Italians drink them, and generally I prefer a Vermouth or dry Sherry before meals. But neither of those goes well with soda, and in the Italian summer climate one very often feels that a plain short drink will not help the thirst one has developed. Taking into consideration the English taste I cannot unconditionally recommend the various *Bitter Campari, Bianco Sarti,* and other *Cocktail Bitters.* Yet poured over a lump of ice and with a fair dash of soda water they are pleasant, refreshing drinks in the heat. A small quantity of any of them mixed in a cocktail is also very good. Their level of alcohol is kept somewhat lighter than the usual strength of most liqueurs.

VII

'When in Rome, do as the Romans do'.

When you are in Rome and have to cross a street, look for a mother—preferably with a number of children—and join them. You might prefer to walk miles to the next guarded crossing—but if you do not, believe me, this is the only safe way across. Even when the traffic is at its fastest and most murderous, children are not run over. Mothers pushing a pram offer you an extra feeling of security—the pram seems to act as a sort of spearhead into the ceaseless onrush of cars and buses.

When in Rome, and meal times come, watch for a priest and hang on to him! Follow him wherever he leads you. You will not have to look for more than a minute . . . Eternal Rome, the City of the Popes, is full of priests, and most of them are there on brief visits and must eat out. Priests know where to eat well and inexpensively. Not the young ones, please—those have little experience, and even less money to spend than you have, but a nice, plump priest of middle-age whould be an ideal guide to a good *trattoria,* where the food and the wine is excellent and cheap.

Certainly this method is not likely to lead you to "Alfredo Imperatore", opposite the Augustus Mausoleum, where Alfredo, the King of Noodles (so crowned by Douglas Fairbanks and Mary Pickford) makes a show of his *fettucine* and *crêpe suzette.* His is the unchallenged best restaurant in Rome, but I never know who can afford to eat there. I was taken by friends a couple of times, and have been wondering ever since how they managed to pay the bill. However, they did manage, and certainly the mere sight of Alfredo, now in his seventies, mixing a salad or deftly arranging vegetables around a plate of roast, not to speak of the food itself, is worth quite a lot of money.

There is also another Alfredo in Rome, "Alfredo Innocenzi", opposite the beautiful church of Santa Maria in Trastevere, where one can eat at a price more in keeping with an average purse. They could charge much more than they actually do, and it would still be worth sitting there after dinner, with your eyes on the glittering *façade* of the church, across the dimly lit *piazza,* when the golden mosaics shine under the soft sky of the southern night.

We owe it to Rome that wine is ours to-day. Egyptian hieroglyphs, the inscriptions on the bricks of old Babylon, carry many references to viticulture. Wine was mentioned frequently in the Old Testament. Wine vessels from Crete testify to its place in her Minoan civilization. Greek mythology has it that the God Dionysius—Bacchus in Latin—brought the vine from India, of all places. From Greece it spread to Southern Italy, and to Rome. And the Romans, in their conquest of Europe, carried the cultivation of vines wherever their legions set foot.

Wine seems to flow towards Rome from the wide expanse of hills in the distance. From the open osterias of the Via Appia with their stone-tables and stone-benches, to the smoky taverns along both banks of the Tiber, from the countless rosticcerias with their open fires to the white table-clothed restaurants of elegant Rome, there is one ever-recurring symbol of well-being: the sparkling decanters of smooth, blond wine . . *Frascati.*

Is it really all *Frascati?* If it were, the sculptured marble heads, the fishes and tritons and horns of plenty on the fountains of Rome would have to spray jets of wine, instead of water. But nearly all the wine drunk in Rome is *Castelli Romani,* of which *Frascati* is just one, probably the best, variety.

The *Castelli Romani* wines come from the hills south-east of Rome, beyond Ciampino airport, where Rome's patricians of the Renaissance built their summer villas. *Colli Albani, Velletri* (you may remember the place in connection with the Anzio beach-head), *Colli Lanuviani, Colonna,* and *Marino,* are, after *Frascati,* the best known qualities. Yet one is well advised not to insist on any of them in particular. Either your choice happens to be the choice of the restaurant, when you will receive it anyway, just by ordering *un quarto bianco;* or if it is not, then the waiter will not say a word and just appear with what he has and put it in front of you as though it were the one you asked for. As all the varieties are equally good, there is no real need for specification. *Un quartino, un mezzo, un litro, due litri* are the measures which you may want to have ready on your tongue: half a pint, one pint, one quart, or two.

Many odes were sung in old Roman days to the praise of the wines from the Albano hills. All the *Castelli Romani* wines are medium (11% to 13%) alcoholic, distinguished by a pleasant fruity bouquet, and have a slightly sweet aroma; within their basic demi-sec quality, some tend more towards a dry taste, some are more on the semi-sweet side. They are usually served fairly young; but if one restaurant carries on its wine-list one of those specific names I have given, it will probably be a somewhat older vintage of which the host is rightly proud.

Frascati (its proper vintage name is really *Cannellino*) may be the one exception in this otherwise fairly even field. It is outstanding for its topaz colour, its liveliness, and its higher level of about 13% alcohol. Also, it ages

58

extremely well, and in certain memorable years there exist perfectly dry *Frascatis*—called extra-dry for good measure—which are really brilliant.

The Italians are not very fussy about vintage years . . . wines are good or bad, excellent or not so good, and it is hard to single out a particular year of one growth or the other. To the Italians, wine is a matter of enjoyment, rather than an awesome cult. Their praise is spectacularly descriptive rather than related to such dry facts as dates of years. "Try it and you will agree that it is simply marvellous", is, they find, a better recommendation than sober figures of vintages.

Probably the most imaginative advertising I ever heard was that of a farmer from whom I was about to buy some wine which I had just sampled and praised. I knew his farmlands inside and out, having lived in the district for some time, and wanted to know from which of his various vineyards this wine came. "It does not come from any vineyard", he replied with gentle reproach. "This wine was pee'd by the angels".

The famous *Malvasia* ('drowned in a butt of Malmsey') seems to have been much more popular in past centuries than it is now. Apart from that, *Malvasia* is not red, as we usually picture it, but a light golden yellow. The Roman variety is grown on the hills of Grottaferrata, near Frascati, and frequently sold under the common heading of *Castelli Romani* with the others of that name, and indeed there is no remarkable difference, although the vine is a different one, that is, the "Malvasia", whereas the other wines of the hills of Rome come mainly from "Trebbiano" vines.

There are some more *Malvasia* districts farther south in Lucania and Apulia, but I do not think their *Malvasia* quite comes up to the quality of the Roman variety.

And an excellent *passito* type, very sweet and strongly alcoholic, is the speciality of the Stromboli islands: *Malvasia di Lipari.*

As the white wines of Rome are very generous in taste it does not matter much that good red wines, which you may usually prefer with a meat course, are not always available. Anyhow, in the hot Roman summer, light meat dishes are preferable to the heavier red meats, and the Romans are masters in their preparation. One should also bear in mind that white wine is much more refreshing than red.

What red wine there is, mostly comes from Frosinone, half way between Rome and Cassino, the *Cesanese del Piglio,* a very strong (up to 15%), dark ruby-red wine, of very aromatic flavour, rarely perfectly dry, rather with a warm, sweet tinge.

The cherry-red *Cerasuolo,* grown in the district of Aquila in the Abbruzzi mountains, is much lighter, a nice, delicate wine, on the sweet side; but in that leisurely atmosphere of sunshine, palm trees, blossoming oleanders, and marble columns and arches, it is quite acceptable also as a table wine.

If you really want to know what *Castelli Romani* and especially *Frascati* wine is, it might be a good idea to spend a day going from Rome into the surrounding countryside. The Albano hills are very beautiful, with their little lakes set like blue eyes deep amidst green woods, vineyards and olive groves. There are lots of little restaurants everywhere, whether you go to Rocca di Papa, the Lake Albano, the Lake Nenni, or Frascati (the Tusculum of ancient Rome), and it is a happy experience to see the host descend into his deep cellar and return with your wine . . . a fresh veil of dew appears upon the decanter as soon as it emerges from the ice-cool depths into the warmth above.

You nibble green, raw *fave* (broad beans) while you wait for your lunch, which takes a little while because everything is freshly cooked. You will have become hungry and thirsty, and I should warn you to be cautious with the glittering wine put before you—otherwise another quality of the *Frascati* will reveal itself: *Frascati* is treacherous, the Romans say. It tastes so light and fragrant, you feel you can drink it like water, but therein lies the deception.

I was once at Castelgandolfo with a couple from London whom I had met in Rome and two Italian friends who took us to their favourite restaurant. All was perfectly normal until after the fruit and coffee. Then, first SHE, a very prim lady, extremely correct in everything she does, turned round from her chair to lie down on what appeared to be the remnants of a Roman wall —just for a second, still taking part in the conversation. After five minutes, HE got up (a very considerate businessman, who always knows precisely what he wants) to fetch a deck-chair for his wife . . . and came back with two: one for himself. After ten more minutes he asked whether I could arrange for a room for them to rest for an hour or so. It was the heat, of course——

*　　　*　　　*

Rome's other main source of wine is centred at Orvieto and Montefiascone, near the Lake of Bolsena.

Est Est Est, the wine of Montefiascone, owes its name to a bishop who used to send his quartermaster on ahead when he travelled; the man had orders to chalk a mark "Est" (short for *vinum bonum est*) on the doors of those inns which he found suitable for the bishop. The wine of Montefiascone so impressed the quartermaster that he could not recommend it with one "Est" only, and wrote it three times instead. Usually the story ends there, but sometimes it goes on to tell that the bishop, when he arrived, was so much in agreement with the opinion of his quartermaster that he decided to stay there for the rest of his life.

I do not know if he did, but at any rate I am not quite in agreement with him. *Est Est Est* is very similar to the *Castelli Romani* wines, somewhat lighter (10 to 12% alcoholic content), and tends more towards sweetness than they do. However, it is only fair to point out that owing to its pretty name a lot of it is exported, and certainly *Est Est Est* with its golden yellow colour is not a bad choice.

To *Orvieto* (usually bottled in low-bottomed flasks, similar to the wicker flasks of *Chianti*) I give my unqualified support. *Orvieto* is a very charming wine, the dry quality up to 13% of alcohol, the semi-sweet (*amabile* or *abboccato*) type around 11%. Both are preciously delicate wines, with an almost ethereal aroma. I do not think that even the dry *Orvieto* is ever so perfectly dry as some other wines may be, but what sweetness it has is well balanced by a slightly bitter after-taste.

It is widely maintained that the cellars, cut deep into the tuff rock of Orvieto, play a great part in the delicacy of the wine. It is obtained from "Trebbiano" grapes which we find again and again in Italy, and always in connection with the best wines; here they seem to have brought forth a particularly delicious variation. One should not choose *Orvieto* as a table wine for any and every meal; it should be a companion only to food as delicate as the wine itself.

* * *

Few wines have ever stimulated the imagination as much as the three connected with Naples: *Falerno, Lacrima Christi,* and *Capri.* And few names are more apt than those to awaken in the mind the image of brilliant sunshine, colourful living, and the endless expanse of a shimmering blue sea beneath a cerulean sky. I only wish the wines of Naples could really compare in quality with the beauty of the landscape!

To begin with, *Capri* is a wine which hardly exists. When it is to be found, it is a pleasant, well-balanced, dry white wine, of medium strength, with a fresh, fragrant bouquet. It is exactly the sort of wine one expects the wine of the island of Capri to be, but I doubt if one finds it outside the cellar of an individual grower, or perhaps at the home of one of the few people who are lucky enough to choose Capri as their residence. It is quite impossible that the hundreds of thousands of bottles of *Capri* served at the tables of Capri's hotels, and shipped all over the world from Cairo to Manhattan, really contain wine from the few vineyards of Capri and Anacapri.

In the small local osterias you are much more likely to come at least fairly near to the original produce. They will probably serve wine from the same vines, "Greco" and "Fiano", though grown near Sorrento and in Ischia. This wine is very much the same thing as *Capri,* but its qualities are not as pronounced as they should be. Otherwise, what passes as *Capri* under those pretty fancy labels mostly comes from the main land near Naples. This is not to say that those are necessarily bad wines— they are just not *Capri.* Some of them, mostly from the hill land beyond Caserta, are quite good, *Ravello,* for instance, *Solopaca, Greco di Tuffo,* and *Fiano di Avellino.* Not all growths of these varieties are identical; more often than not the wines tend to be on the sweet side.

Nor is there much chance of having the often mentioned red *Capri*. There is even less of it in existence than of the white one. What often passes for it is really the light wine of Naples, the *Vesuvio*. Though at times it may be somewhat rough, it is a good wine for its price —in the osterias of Bella Napoli. Bottled, and labelled, and priced as *Capri* it becomes an entirely different proposition.

The southern slopes of Mt. Vesuvius are the birthplace of *Lacrima Christi*, which stands among the wines of Italy best known on all foreign markets. Cultivated on "Greco" and "Fiano" vines, it is a near relative of *Capri*, but has not quite its charm. *Lacrima Christi* is an excellent wine by all standards, though its renown seems to exceed its qualities. There is one rather intriguing feature about it: it is a white wine that should not be served very cool, but slightly *chambrée*. Incidentally, red *Lacrima Christi*, although it is little known, is equally admirable with the white variety.

Legend has woven a very pretty story around *Lacrima Christi*. It is said that when Lucifer was thrown out of Heaven he managed to grasp a small piece of Paradise, and took it with him; as he fell into the sea his little piece of Paradise created what is now the Gulf of Naples. But one day Christ saw the sins that thrived even in this Paradise on earth, and shed a tear over the wickedness of Man. It fell upon a vineyard and the grapes have grown richer and fuller ever since.

Falerno, of course, has been famous from olden times. Horace is there behind every glass of *Falerno*, inviting us to join him in his praise of the wine. The shadows of Capua and Pompeii tell us of Roman feasts under the stars of warm summer nights. In Roman times, *Falerno* was a red wine. The *Falerno* we drink to-day is a white variety, a delicate, golden wine, semi-dry, of medium strength. Red *Falerno* has lost its distinction. The production is centred around Formia and Mondragone, on the hills between the Liri and Volturno rivers, so well and so unhappily known to us for the long fighting in 1943.

However, if you ask me for my preference among the Neapolitan wines—it is *Gragnano*, without a second's hesitation. Is it only the rich purple hue that fascinates me? Or perhaps the idea that it is grown upon the steep hills between Sorrento, Amalfi and Castellamare? It may be that I always like those wines best which are not similar to any other wine elsewhere. *Gragnano* is unconventionally light for a red wine. This may account for its mellow taste—so mellow, in fact, that one can hardly realize if one is drinking the dry *Gragnano* or the *abboccato*.

Gragnano and candle light are both responsible for an odd little adventure I had in Naples in the last year of the war. I had drunk quite a lot of *Gragnano* in the small, dark wine-bar off San Biagio, and the lights of the candles in the rough iron-stands fell upon a solitary and rather melancholy drinker who had to leave Naples, lovely city of lovers, early next morning. When the young man with his portfolio of drawings approached me, I was not in the least interested in the idea of looking at them. But I was alone and a little nostalgic and probably because it was past midnight and he seemed tired and dejected, I offered him a drink, which he accepted. We finished a small bottle, and then a second, when he said: "Do you want to see a drawing by Matisse?"

Of course I did. It was a sketch, one of his ballerinas,

not superb, but very good. He told me a story of an Italian count who had evacuated his collection from Naples after the first bombing, and then died. He himself was the best friend of the old count's grandson, who needed some ready money quickly. (More probably, he needed capital to go into the black market!) His price was extremely modest, but I had only just enough money for another bottle or two of wine.

The bar—just a few shaky tables and chairs polished with age—was empty but for the two of us and the *padrone*. "Want to look at my pictures?" my companion repeated. "I can show you an Utrillo, very cheap, ridiculously cheap". White houses in a harbour, one or two boats—it seemed an Utrillo to me. And his Braque was similar to the one I had seen in Paris years ago, and his Chagall carried the perfume, so to speak, of the gay twenties, and his Toulouse-Lautrec was a girl from a cabaret and had yellow hair and a cheeky uptilted nose. He was proud of his collection, and in a way I was proud to see it, and we became very friendly while I admired a colourful South-Sea painting by Gauguin in the light of the flickering candles. It all seemed rather unreal, and when I told him that I was unable to buy even the smallest of his pictures, he did not seem to mind.

Suddenly he gave me a charming grin and said: "Of course, I have painted them all myself. They are fakes. But they are the best fakes you can buy in Europe". I must have looked astonished, for he laughed. "I can do Turner, too, and Henri Rousseau, he is my speciality, but they are too big to carry about. They go to the art galleries".

I was not sure what to believe; was the count and his grandson an invention? He shrugged his shoulders. "I tell you, I paint them myself. I tell you, because I am drunk. And you are drunk, too, and you are my friend and you understand that an artist must live". I understood everything and nothing at this hour. My friend brought me home, and we shook hands for a long time in a dark street in Naples, before parting for ever. I do not know if I came across one of the best forgers of modern pictures that night, or whether the *Gragnano* charmed my eyes into seeing masterpieces in crude simple drawings. Or was it that he made fun of me when he saw I would not buy, and all his sketches were in fact genuine? Perhaps the *Gragnano* knows, I don't. It was a very good evening all the same.

VIII

If it be true that I do think,
There are five reasons why men drink.
Good wine, a friend, or being dry,
Or least we should be bye and bye,
Or any other reason why.

(Henry Aldrich, 1647—1710).

Other vine-growing districts of Italy may forgive me if I
dedicate too much space, and perhaps an overdose of
enthusiasm to Piedmont, and to Turin in particular. I
cannot even excuse myself by saying that I have more
friends there than in other places of Italy. It is just that
I like the town immensely.

Turin has a graceful solidity of character, and a strong
French influence even in its more humble buildings.
Turin is not so bursting with activity as Milan, it is not
so proud as Florence, it lacks the sumptuousness of
Rome. To sum up: Turin has elegance. So have the
wines of Piedmont.

The smaller provincial places also have a certain quiet
distinction. Like Turin, they are somewhat remote from
the rush of the *Americanismo Novecento* now sported
all over Italy. The noisier sides of the Italian character
are absent here—or, if not quite absent, at any rate less
conspicuous. The lovely hills on the right bank of the
river Po look peacefully down into the streets of Turin,
and a few minutes' bus ride brings you from the centre
of the town to green meadows and quiet woods. Regard-
less of the potential power of their engines, buses and
cars proceed at a pace which allows pedestrians the
possibility of crossing a road.

With an undertone of malice, however strongly mixed with envy, other Italians call Turin the most Italian town of France. It is not for nothing that it was Piedmont which, not so long ago, set out to challenge the French in the production of Champagne.

It is understood that one should not really say "Champagne", for Champagne can never be anything else but the strongly sparkling wine which comes from the French district of that name. Indeed the Italians, or the Piedmontese for that matter, after first calling their sparkling wine "Asti Champagne", "Moscato Champagne", and "Champagne Italiano", have for some time now introduced the names "Spumante" and "Asti Spumante", and quite rightly so: *Spumante,* good as it is, is not Champagne.

I believe that the initial idea of letting the Italian sparkling wine profit by the name "Champagne", using it as though it were merely synonymous for "sparkling", has done the *Spumante* more harm than good. It created a bias against it, logical perhaps though unjustified, a bias which to a great extent has lasted until the present day. *Asti Spumante* can hold its own so long as it stands on its own merits and conveys the idea of all the loveliness of Italy translated into sparkling bubbles. As soon as one forces on it a comparison with Champagne, the *Spumante* will invariably lose for the simple reason that it has no such vintages as those which built up the overwhelming fame of the French *cuvées.* One has heard so much of these, that one automatically compares the *Asti Spumante* not with the ordinary "No Vintage" Champagne such as you come by more frequently, but with the famous *Pommery 1892* of King Edward VII

The commercial production of sparkling *Moscato* was first begun about one hundred years ago in the district of Asti, by one big grower who adopted the classical French *Champenoise* technique for processing the sweet *Moscato* wines. Nearly all the production of white sparkling wine, sweet and dry, still has its home in the district of Asti. On a more simple, rural level, the practice of producing sweet sparkling wines is much older, however, and is known in many other places where suitable grapes exist, especially in the North.

Any vine-growing farmer in the Po Valley will at a given time, with a funny, secretive expression on his face, take samples from the various barrels of new wine in his cellar, and perhaps mutter: "This one might be the thing. Let us try". This wine which may be sparkling in the future, is perhaps not the pride of the pater familias, but, rather, his hobby. His pride will always be the solid, well-aged wines, his art will be the selection of the right vintages for maturing. But the sparkling wine experiment—and to the small grower it is a new experiment from year to year—has a good deal of excitement about it. It may succeed, it may not. He will only know when he opens the bottles. Sometimes the cork will come out with a happy pop followed by rich foam, sometimes the wine is just flat, or only mildly effervescent.

The *Champenois* treatment, invented by a French Bénédictine monk, Dom Pérignon, towards the end of the Seventeenth Century, involves a rather complex procedure. It is easy enough to explain—what is really responsible for the millions of tiny bubbles in a sparkling wine? The carbon-dioxyde which develops during the fermentation of the young wine. Normally it evaporates from the barrel. However, if the wine is bottled before the fermentation is completely over, this natural carbonic acid gas cannot escape but remains in the wine until the bottle is opened, then streams out, first in a gush and subsequently slower and slower.

This is quite all right in principle. But if you bottle too early, too much carbon-dioxyde is developed and the whole thing blows up. The big plants have all the technical equipment to test the stage of fermentation for the right moment of bottling. The small grower has to rely on his tongue, and in order to keep on the safe side he will tend to bottling too late rather than too early. It may often happen that there will not be enough ferments left in the new wine to develop a good sparkle.

I came to know the farm-produced *Spumante* during my long stay in the Romagna (the province extending, roughly, between Bologna and Ravenna), and I daresay there cannot be anything lovelier. The best Champagne party cannot compare with the moment you arrive on a hot summer day at a solitary farm cooling itself under a cluster of trees amidst the fields, and the farmer disappears into the cellar and returns with a bottle of his *frizzante*. They do not call it *spumante,* they leave this expression to the big shippers, out of a sense of modesty. But what they pour out is sheer heaven, and puts you immediately at ease; with the first glass you feel that all that goes on outside the short range of your vision is immaterial compared to the peace in your mind. There is the stone bench in front of the house where you sit, there is the farmyard, the hens, the barn, a few shrubs, bushes, and trees, and this is all there is of the world.

There is one thing the farmers cannot achieve with their *frizzante*. It is quite impossible for them to carry out the proper *dégorgement* which would eliminate the sediment that has settled in the bottle during the fermentation. Thus, the sediment remains at the bottom of the bottle, and one must be careful not to pour it out

71

with the wine. It does no real harm to the taste of the wine, but it is no asset to the wine's appearance. Nor can any bottle be emptied completely; the last glass or so will always have to be left. Obviously this farmhouse *vino frizzante* would not be "safe" enough for marketing —it might go out of condition while being stored. But in any case, it is not for sale. The farmers produce it only for their own pleasure.

For the production of the great *Spumante* wines, particular care must be taken with the harvest, the selection, and the pressing of the grapes. The carbon-dioxyde which breaks up during the fermentation and remains caught within the wine, enlivens its bouquet and aroma; in the same way it would also act to reveal the slightest flaws caused by imperfect grapes.

As soon as the first stage of fermentation is over, the wine is bottled in extra-strong bottles which can resist the pressure of the carbon-dioxyde, and now the most costly procedure begins: the task of separating the sediment, which consists chiefly of mineral salts. This process is long, involved, and expensive. Skilled labour is costly, and the natural fermentation in the bottle, as it is called, calls for a lot of skill—reason enough why sparkling wines cost so much more than any other wine.

The bottles are first stacked flat for several months, then transferred onto trestle-like racks, called *pupitres*, where they rest in a slanting position, with their necks pointing downwards, so that the sediment settles round the cork. The whole process from harvest to finishing takes about five years to complete, partly also because, under the pressure of the carbon-dioxyde and cut off from the outside air, the fermentation only proceeds very slowly. During all their time on the *pupitres* the bottles, millions of them stacked in endless rows in the long vaults of the cellars, are continuously controlled, cautiously rotated, gently shaken to loosen the sediment which clings to their sides, their slanting position lowered. How the *remneurs* who do that work know the exact moment when one of these manifold moves has to be made, I cannot comprehend, and I think it is beyond the understanding of anyone who has not grown up in the trade. When I look at these bottles all I can see is greenish glass with some liquid inside. But these men seem to see what stage of fermentation the wine in every single bottle has reached. They have "the feel of the skilled hand"—which is just another way of expressing what one cannot explain. And yet, for all the painstaking attention, the mortality rate during the second fermentation is very high. Every now and then the pop of an exploding bottle rings through the cool cellars—another contributing cause to the high cost of the wine.

Finally the great moment arrives—the *dégorgement*. The bottles are opened: the sediment which has accumulated in the neck shoots out with a gush of foam, and immediately the cork is secured again. It is the skill of the *dégorgeur* to execute this operation so quickly that as little as possible of the wine is lost. What is lost is replaced either by a measure of the same wine, or with the *dosage*—a mixture of very old wine, sugar, and brandy, to regulate the degree of sweetness and strength. The *Spumante* is ready for dispatch.

According to the *dosage*, the finished *Spumante* will be either:

"demi-sec", that is, in practice, fairly sweet, or

"dry" which to all practical purposes still means slightly sweet, or

"extra-dry" which in fact signifies dry with a touch of sweetness, or "brut"—the stamp of the really extra-dry (to my taste over-dry) quality.

This classification may sound bewildering to us, as it does not conform to our usual notion of sweet and dry. However, it has been established by international custom and means in fact that by nature sparkling wine requires some measure of sweetness. Thus, a taste which would be considered as sweet for ordinary wine, is still qualified as dry with sparkling wines.

The Italian *Spumante* production started originally with the indigenous sweet *Asti Spumante*, based on the *Moscato* grapes of the Asti district. Only at a later stage did the Italians introduce the French "Pinot" vines from the Champagne and begin to process their own "dry" *Spumante* wines, closely following the French pattern of production. So French, indeed, is this pattern that the terminology has remained entirely French.

Although most of the imported "Pinots" are equally cultivated in the district of Asti, where they thrive very well indeed, the "dry" *Spumante* qualities carry only the name of the shipper and the word "Spumante", without "Asti". The name "Asti Spumante" is only given to the *Moscato* produce processed in the true *Champenoise* technique. However, for some reason or other, the word "Moscato" is generally omitted from the label. Perhaps it is indeed better reserved for the "still" *Moscato,* which certainly is as much a class by itself as *Asti Spumante.*

I do not want to make this explanation too cumbersome, but I believe that I ought to indicate at least some instances.

Cinzano classify their produce "Spumante Cinzano Dry"—'Extra Dry"—"Brut"—and "Riserva" which is demi-sec, apart from the sweet "Asti Spumante Cinzano".

Gancia, at Canelli, in the heart of the Asti district, say

"Gancia Asti Spumante" for the sweet *Moscato* produce; "Riserva Reale" for demi-sec; "Gran Spumante" for dry; "Riserva", with the year of vintage for extra-dry.

Contratto, a smaller firm, also of Canelli, label "Asti Spumante" as the others do, but "Gran Spumante" for extra-dry.

Martini and Rossi, world famous for their huge production of Vermouths, also venture into this field. They have "Asti Spumante" and an excellent dry "Gran Spumante".

Marchesi-Antinori, principal shippers of *Orvieto*, and equally well known for their Chianti production, also stake their name on the "Pinot" vines and produce one "Gran Spumante Secco"—dry, and one "Spumante Dolce"—sweet.

Equally outside the Asti district are Ferrari, at Trento, in the Alto Adige, where "Pinots" become generally more and more popular with the growers. They ship "Ferrari Secco"—dry, "Gran Spumante Ferrari"— demi-sec, the extra-dry "Riserva", and a *"brut"* quality. They all catch the eye with a marked tinge of green to their extremely light colour.

It is very difficult to state preferences. I do not think there are really overwhelming differences in quality. Of the *Asti Spumante* wines, which are my choice before any other, Gancia is probably the best. For *"brut"* I might select Cinzano. Marchesi-Antinori are usually very happy with the choice of their "dry" vintages. Of the Martini types also I prefer the "dry" one. For demi-sec and extra dry I would go back to Gancia.

You see, I am partial to *Spumante,* with my heart open to all the varying *finesses* the different makers create. Still, I should not dare to grade the Italian *Spumante* wines as on a level with Champagne. But they are without doubt of incomparably higher quality than the widely known sparkling moselles, burgundies, and hocks, which in general are taken much more seriously. Besides, in the *(Moscato) Asti Spumante* Italy has a wine in a class entirely apart.

Unlike the French Champagne, whose cost is additionally steeped in prestige value, the Italian *Spumante* is no extravagance. Over here, the difference in price is not so remarkable, because the price picture is blurred by the heavy duty which is clamped alike on both. But when we are in Italy, where the Italians consider a bottle of *Spumante* as a natural thing to have, we need not baulk at the expense. Nor need we wait for a special "occasion". Certainly, *Spumante* is more—much more—expensive than even the very best table wines—partly because one drinks it so quickly and easily; but then, it is a wine which gives so much gay pleasure.

Of course, its unique character lies essentially in the fact that it foams and sparkles. But does all its charm merely come from those myriads of dancing bubbles? Is it only those that make one's imagination fly? They add a lot to the wine, they evoke all its fragrance. And it is certain that they create a kind of festive atmosphere. *Spumante* is a wine to enhance every meal from the first course to the last, as well as the best aperitif ever thought of, the most pleasant of all dessert wines, and the best drink quite on its own, at whatever time of the day—or night. Last but not least, it is a drink no woman will ever decline. I do not know why it is, but every woman invariably likes it on its merits as a wine, and not only on the instinctive feeling that it flatters her beyond measure.

IX

Of the vine-growing districts of Italy, Piedmont is the most important for the quality as well as for the extent of its production. The whole Italian output, in a good year, reaches 48 to 50 million hectolitres (22 gallons to one hectolitre), of which about six million come from Piedmont, and more than four and a half from Tuscany. Only Apulia shows a higher figure, nearly 7 million hectolitres, but the great bulk of Apulian wines is of lower quality, whereas in Piedmont as well as in Tuscany there is hardly a wine that would not count at least as a good table wine.

Apart from the *Moscato* and *Spumante* wines of Asti, three other wines are outstanding among the wide range of Piedmontese: *Barolo, Barbera,* and *Dolcetto.* They are all red, or rather what the Italians like to call *vino nero*—"black". And of these *Barolo* is certainly the best wine of Piedmont, and probably the best wine of Italy —possibly also the most expensive one. The Turinese become quite romantic even when they mention it, and there is an affectionate gleam in their eyes when they speak of their *Re dei vini*—their "king of wines". Poetic feelings apart, this is indeed a regal wine; it has something which I can best characterize with the expression: it has so much style.

It was a very "stylish" occasion, too, when I first met *Barolo,* in the home of one of the leading vermouth makers of Turin. He lives in a "villa" surrounded by a big park on the hillside not far from the town: a fair sized Eighteenth Century *palais,* the sort of thing we use to pay half a crown to visit streaming through on a guided tour of one of the stately homes of England.

The *barocco piemontese* is an extremely beautiful style, which makes a lavish use of mirrors in the interiors, and is somehow more colourful and nearer to earth than the French Baroque, splendid enough though not so imperial. I must confess that I felt a little shy when faced with all that architectural grandeur as a setting for dinner, and I must still apologize to Mr. Turati and his beautiful young wife that I probably spoke far too little of his vermouth, on which I wanted some information, and far too much of everything else, *Barolo* and *Dolcetto* included. However, I was set at ease not only by my charming hosts and by their wines, but also by the two dogs who played happily around the dinner table in front of the house, careering over the gravel and right through the roses. We dined to the accompaniment of cicadas and against the background of a neat defile of trees emerging into the starlight from the darkness of the park. I am not quite sure now if the actual reality of that evening did not make it seem still more unreal.

Back to the hard facts about *Barolo*: the ground on which it grows is tufa again—of which we heard in connection with Orvieto—very hard for the vines to set root in. Yet we see this generally in viticulture; hill-wine is always better than wine from the plain, and the more difficult the terrain, the harder the vine has to work in order to tap the resources of the soil for the growing grapes, the better the wine will be.

The *Barolo* grape needs the first autumn mists to develop its full flavour. Of the prime quality of the wine, which probably beats any of its best French rivals, there are perhaps a few thousand bottles a year, just from one hill. But in general, *Barolo* is the produce of the vineyards of ten villages of which the village of

Barolo is the centre, situated in the province of Cuneo where the hill-land rises steeply towards the Ligurian and Maritime Alps. Each of these will have some 1,500 hectolitres a year. I should estimate that at least one third of it is consumed locally; in other words, *Barolo* is in very limited supply.

I have as yet to meet a wine which is so full in body and still without the slightest trace of heaviness. The gradation of the best growths accounts for 15% of alcohol, with a minimum of 14% for the others. With its bouquet reminiscent of violets, *Barolo* has a very rare aromatic quality, and is very soft and velvety on the palate. The growers manage the wine with great care and never issue any of it before it is five or six years old. *Barolo* must be old to be good, they say, and maintain that the young wine hardly resembles the old. Indeed, it is remarkable to observe how steadily the wine progresses with the years, with practically no limit to its optimum, and though this is only an outward feature it is fascinating to see the golden shades this typically dark wine acquires with age. I prefer *Barolo* with the second or third course of a meal rather than at the beginning, and like to linger over it long after the last crumb has been consumed.

Although we may be able to scrutinize the technicalities and to analyze chemically the influences which bring about a good wine here and a bad wine elsewhere, we are still at a loss to understand how nature works to make one particular wine so superior. All we know is that within the small bounds of the zone of Barolo, nature has contrived to combine some ideal elements.

A few miles away, there is a wine, a near relative to the *Barolo,* grown on the hillside stretching towards Alba, which is called *Barbaresco* after the central town of this region, and is cultivated on the same vine, the "Nebbiolo". The *Barbaresco* possesses a good measure of the essential features of the other, including the appearance of an orange glimmer on the dark colour of the wine in its more advanced years; yet they are present in a much less distinguished way.

Somehow or other, the elements which form the unique quality of the *Barolo* are not so well integrated to a smooth compound, and there is certainly no question of putting the *Barbaresco* on a level with its nobler brother. I like it immensely, as a very good and always interesting table wine of great character and full taste. On the whole, it is perhaps slightly coarser and, with an alcoholic content of about 13%, somewhat lighter. It comes to maturity much sooner but is well worth good aging. Its production area is roughly equal in size or only slightly larger, than that of the *Barolo*.

The "Nebbiolo" vine is widely cultivated all over Piedmont, and generally produces very pleasant, acceptable table wines which are usually sold fairly young as *Nebbiolo*. They are mostly lighter in colour than the two I mentioned before, and also less alcoholic, about 12 per cent. Their main quality lies in their pleasingly fresh taste. Nearly all of them carry a rather pronounced prickle *(frizzantino)*, which in some of them is very nearly *mousseux* and is combined with a very agreeable, more or less pointed touch of sweetness. This makes *Nebbiolo* more advisable as an accompaniment to lighter meat dishes, particularly poultry, than to roast, red meat in general, or to pork. However much I like this prickly demi-sec *Nebbiolo*, I find it a mistake to carry this tendency of the wine to the point of making it straightforward sweet and sparkling, as some growers, or shippers, do.

The "Nebbiolo" grape (*nebbia* signifies "mist" in Italian) is the last to be harvested everywhere. Its vinous characteristics change easily, almost from slope to slope. It would be useless to seek in the common *Nebbiolo*, likeable as it is, any definite affinity to its two principal species, the *Barolo* and the *Barbaresco*. But there are two more regional growths of the same vine, equally limited in quantity, which also stand out for their special characteristics. One can easily recognize both by their clear red colour. The *Carema* is a very lively wine with a well distinguished bouquet, almost harsh when young, which makes it an ideal wine to go with pork. The *Gattinara* is more refined, also perfectly dry, with a somewhat tarry background. Neither is likely to be much stronger than 11% of alcohol.

I should accord the second place in Piedmont's vinous glory to the *Dolcetto*. If my readers have already noticed my sweet tooth and may be inclined to reproach me for it, I hasten to say that, though linguistically *dolcetto* means "slightly sweet", the wine is not. Warning should be given, however, that there exists also a Sicilian *Dolcetto* which is indeed sweet, or semi-sweet.

The Piedmontese *Dolcetto* is again a very dark wine, the sort of colour typified by the Italian expression *vino nero*. Perfectly smooth, with a most delicate bouquet, extremely harmonious and velvety in taste, this charming wine comes easily into a class with some of the very best French appellation wines. It is rather on the lighter side of the scale, measuring between 10 and 12 per cent of alcoholic content, a wine of great elegance which is at its best advantage at the beginning of a meal. The idea of calling it, as well as the grape and the vine, *dolcetto* may have been suggested by its unusually moderate acidity. The various growths do not differ widely one from the other; "delle Langhe" and "d'Ovada" are those you see most. The prime breed, however, is the one called "Dogliani", which comes from only a few miles away from Barolo, from the estate of the former president of the Italian republic, Luigi Einaudi.

Piedmont's favourite wine is the *Barbera*. The "Barbera" vine, very robust and virile, thrives easily nearly everywhere all over Piedmont, but the best and richest sites are those of Asti, in the first place, Cuneo, and Alessandria. So popular indeed is the *Barbera* that its production accounts for over one million hectolitres, about one fifth of the total production of the many wines of Piedmont. And it well deserves its popularity. *Barbera* is already an excellent wine in its second year, and becomes better with every year it is allowed to mature. It is a full-bodied, dark red wine, starting with an alcoholic level of 12 per cent and going to 15, dry and firm, very vinous in flavour and much coarser than the other red Piedmontese. It is typically the wine to welcome you to Piedmont. Quite a lot of it is available in England, usually of good quality. Why some growers, or merchants insist on producing it, or having it produced, in an *amabile* type—that is, semi-sweet, and even *frizzante*, is beyond my understanding. Of course, it is easy enough to manage the fermentation in such a way that the wine retains some sugar and some effervescence; but *Barbera*, with its basically austere character, is certainly not the wine for it.

It seems unnecessary, too, in a country like Piedmont which can satisfy this otherwise very agreeable trend of taste with the excellent *Freisa*, which so to speak cries out to be allowed to be sweet and sparkling. Some of the best "Freisa" vines grow on the hills of Chieri near Turin. When dry and too young—not every *Freisa* is thought worthy of the more careful treatment—this deep red wine can be rather harsh on the palate. Certainly there are one or two perfect *Freisa Secco* wines, but primarily it lends itself marvellously to becoming a moderately alcoholic, slightly sparkling wine (what the French call *pétillant*), semi-sweet, with a tempting aroma of strawberries. Recommended for easy-going wine parties alfresco style!

On the same lines, but on a more distinguished level, are the *Bonarda*, the *Brachetto*, and the *Grignolino*, all grown on that endless expanse of hills spreading from the town of Asti towards the high mountains far in the distance. Unfortunately, the "Grignolino" vine is now nearly extinct; on one vineyard after the other the growers see the vine deteriorate, as though it had exhausted its span of life, and are forced to abandon its cultivation.

The other two are cultivated only on a small scale. *Bonarda* is a dark red, fresh and harmonious wine, slightly sparkling and moderately alcoholic. *Brachetto*, with the typical colour of cherries, also sparkling and on a level of not more than 10% of alcohol, is definitely on the sweet side, an exquisite, mellow dessert wine. The few *Grignolino* wines that still exist are undoubtedly the best of the three. Dry, with a slightly bitter tang and high alcoholic level, the wine is quite interesting to try, but I rather prefer the very attractive semi-sweet and *pétillant* variety. I think that the Piedmontese speciality of slightly sweet and sparkling red wines, whose light-hearted tendencies contradict so pleasantly the warmer and firmer side of their red wine character, is one of the nicest experiences of the wine-loving traveller in Italy.

With all that enormous range of red wines, good white table wines are the exception in Piedmont. The one that counts comes from a vine called "Cortese"—which, literally translated, means "courteous". Whether in fact the name is merely incidental, or was given on purpose, there could not be a better name for the wine. Most of it appears on the wine lists simply as *Cortese*. Some particularly distinguished breeds are *Castello di Canelli* (in the heart of the district of Asti where all the *Cortese* wines come from), *Castello di Sommariva,* and *Monferrato*. Straw-coloured, with high lights of green, fragrant, dry, and lively, these are light wines of great finesse. *Cortese* should be drunk only slightly matured; all its refinement is already in existence when the wine is still young. One of the best is on the wine list of the "Cucolo" Restaurant in Turin, who have an exclusive agreement with one of the growers.

All over Piedmont the "Moscato" grape gives rise to the production of sparkling *Moscato* wines that are, however, of lesser refinement than those of Asti. A simplified method is applied to them (as to the many semi-sparkling red wines) which is of course much cheaper than the full French technique. This less elaborate procedure—in between the standard *Champenois* and the simple farmhouse treatment—cannot free the wine completely from all sediment. Thus, the sparkling *Moscatos* of that range do not come out as light and brilliant as they should be. On the other hand, if the filtration by which the sediment-forming substances are partly eliminated from the fermenting wine is carried out too stringently, the effervescence of the wine is reduced also.

They are however, extremely nice semi-sweet wines, perhaps more fruity in taste than *Asti Spumante,* and one will not be disappointed in them in spite of their lack of refinement. The producers do not present them in the usual guise of the great *Spumantes,* in order not to encroach upon the rights of the well established *Spumante* making houses, and usually call them *Moscato mousseux,* or *Moscato spumante* with the word "spumante" printed in smaller lettering.

I cannot leave the wines of Piedmont without an eulogy upon the *Caluso,* although owing the the rareness of the wine, this becomes almost an academic statement. Grown in the zone of Caluso (on the way from Turin to the Val d'Aosta), on a particular vine, the "Erbaluce", the *Caluso* is made in an unusual way. The grapes, vintaged at the latest possible date, are spread out on straw mats to dry in the sun and allowed to reach nearly the raisin stage. You can imagine that this involves bringing the mats under cover if it starts raining, and every pair of hands is needed to bring them out again as soon as the rain stops.

Essentially a *passito* wine, of golden yellow colour, it is of high alcoholic degree, at least 14 per cent, and tastes somewhat like sherry. Of its kind it is unique in Italy. It is equalled only by the *vin de paille* ("straw wine") of Arbois in the French Jura—alas! just as rare, if not rarer, than the *Caluso.* In either case, Jura and Piedmont, the wine does not only depend on the special treatment given to the grapes. It is rather that the characteristic quality of the grapes on these particular sites has challenged the growers to develop the method, many hundreds of years ago. And the beauty of this method has not waned since.

X

GOD made Man
   Frail as a bubble;
God made Love,
   Love made Trouble.
God made the Vine,
   Was it a sin
That Man made Wine
   To drown Trouble in?

Oliver Herford: "A Plea"

However interesting the galaxy of Italian wines may seem to the wine lover, commercially the most important produce on foreign markets is vermouth: a blend of wine, pure alcohol, sugar, and aromatic herbs. And a very good and pleasant *apéritif* it is. Perhaps the herbs are responsible for the feeling of relaxation it promotes and for the soothing effect on the nerves.

The history of spiced wines is very old: indeed, nearly as old as wine itself. There is evidence of spiced wines being prepared by Cicero and Hippocrates. Spiced wines were known through the Middle Ages, made at that time with oriental spices such as myrtle, myrrh, almonds, cloves, ginger, sandalwood, and nutmeg. A drink which must have had the essential virtues of our present vermouth seems to have emerged some three hundred years ago in certain districts of Italy—especially Piedmont, Tuscany, and Sicily—and in parts of France, particularly in the Savoie and in Provence, where aromatic herbs of all kinds grew in profusion.

Later on, this home made drink was developed on a more refined level: precious imported spices were added to the local ones, and vermouths were highly favoured by the courts who treasured their recipes as keenly as the recipes of their cooks. It was not until late in the Eighteenth Century that vermouth was produced on an industrial scale. In Italy the industry developed chiefly in Turin, and to-day nearly all Italian vermouth is produced in Piedmont.

Italian vermouth exports amount to over 21 million litres a year. As a comparative figure I may quote the five million bottles of champagne shipped by France to its main customers—England and America. In England, the Italian vermouth is so popular that it accounts for by far the biggest share in the total of all Italian wines imported to the country, the largest individual supplier being Martini's.

The English Martini habit is, I find, altogether a very curious phenomenon. In Italy, if you order a Martini, you get a plain vermouth produced by the firm Martini and Rossi, and that is exactly what you have asked for. If you order a Martini in England, you are served with a drink of half to two thirds gin and a particular dry type of vermouth which may come from any firm, Cinzano, Gancia, a French maker, or indeed even from Martini's. It does not matter which. This coining of a name seems to have come into being because the English idea of mixing gin and vermouth was first tried with French vermouths which are, in general, much drier than the Italian ones. Whereupon the firm Martini and Rossi, already well established at that time with their ordinary vermouths, succeeded in developing a type which was even more dry than the French vermouths, with some particular features which made it an ideal blend with gin.

In consequence, the name of the firm soon became associated with the mixed drink as such, most likely first of all by the barmen. Then the other vermouth producers followed suit and evolved their own super-dry vermouths. Indeed, this extra-dry brand blends so superbly with gin that it is never served on its own; nor should it be: its aromatic flavour of bitter herbs really comes out only when mixed with those additional two parts of gin. On its own, it tastes rather flat.

The opposite gin and vermouth mixture, Gin and It, or Gin and French—two parts of vermouth with one part of gin, is made with sweet vermouth of either country. It must be observed, however, that the French "sweet" vermouth is somewhat drier than the Italian. A classification would run as follows:

Italian white is the sweetest. Of course, the expression "white" is merely conventional, as it is with other wine. It simply means "not red", and in the case of vermouth also "not pale". White vermouth is a bright golden yellow, or at any rate brighter than the dry varieties.

Italian red has approximately the same sugar content, but is made with a stronger emphasis on the bitter aroma. Most "red" vermouths are, strictly speaking, brown rather than red in colour, but with some the red tinge distinctly prevails.

French sweet is distinctly less sweet, but perhaps also less strongly aromatic than the former, and not so dark.

French dry—of pale brown colour.

Italian dry—very pale straw-colour, some with a slightly greenish tinge.

For my palate, the flavour we seek in vermouth is best exemplified by the "red" variety, unmixed, without the addition of any gin. I cannot emphasize this too strongly: red vermouth is a pleasant drink on its own, dry vermouth needs the gin to bring it to life.

Within the "red" range, the possibility of aromatic variations is quite considerable. In the first place, the base wine used in the production of Italian vermouths, the *Moscato,* is a wine with a very clearly defined aroma, and the taste of the final product depends to a great extent on the proportion in which *Moscato* wine is blended with other, mostly dry, wines; it varies between one third to one half.

Secondly, there are, I believe, 59 ingredients out of which the bitter-aromatic infusion is prepared, all sorts of herbs, leaves, plants, flowers, fruits, roots, aromatic woods, barks, dried and ground. The slightest change in the proportion in which they are used, leaving some out altogether and choosing others instead, is apt to bring about quite a distinct variation of the compound flavour. These recipes are closely guarded secrets of the makers, handed down from father to son and professedly known exclusively to the principals of the various firms. But I have the heretical idea that much of this secretiveness is overplayed. There are no two vermouths which do not differ perceptibly from each other, and this is all the better for each of them: any possibility of competition between the various brands (in Italy and France there must be hundreds of them) depends not on similarity, but on the contrary, on their very difference. For instance, for all the international fame of the French vermouths, Italian vermouth is the only foreign wine imported into France. Obviously the true interest of the makers lies in maintaining subtle individual characteristics, not in obtaining each others' secrets, as the big firms would have us believe.

I, for my part, am a great admirer of one particular brand of vermouth: Carpano, but that does not mean that I never drink any other. I am not in sympathy with the habit of refusing everything except three or four favourite drinks and invariably having only these, twice a day, seven days a week, to eternity. In any case, whereas within the classification I have given before all the other brands offer only more or less marginal differences to choose between, Carpano stands in a class apart. Gancia, Mirafiore, Martini, Cinzano, to name the four best known brands, each has a white, red, and a dry variety; if we leave out the dry one, in both the red and the white category Gancia is probably the sweetest, Cinzano the least sweet. I say "probably", because with so many aromatic variations thrown in, it would be difficult to determine what degree of sweetness there is, except by actual chemical analysis.

With Carpano, however, the bitter tang is more sharply pronounced. Though, broadly speaking, it belongs to the "red" category, it is exceptional insofar as no *Moscato* is used as a base wine. There are two kinds, Carpano "Vermouth"—somewhat closer to the usual line of red vermouth, and Carpano "Punt e Mes", with the bitter tang still more emphasized. Indeed, its individuality is so well recognized by Italian bar-tenders that, if you order a vermouth, the barman will serve you any brand he has handy—except Carpano. To have a Carpano you must specifically ask for one of its two varieties by name.

Punt e Mes—"Point and a half"—seems an odd name for a vermouth. The story attached to it goes back to 1786 when Carpano's (incidentally, the first industrial vermouth makers in Italy) opened their own bar in piazza Castello in Turin, next to the Stock Exchange.

Naturally, the bankers and brokers overflowed to the new café to continue business over a glass of vermouth. From the incessant hum of voices negotiating stock quotations, one word continuously impressed itself on the ears of the bar-tenders: *punt e mes*. And when, one day, Carpano's produced a new kind of vermouth with an extra point of bitter aroma, the choice of name was obvious.

The mixing and processing of vermouth is, I find, a most fascinating art—or science, whichever it may be. The main idea is of course the spicing of the wine to obtain an appetizing *apéritif*. The sweetening is only co-related to it, to off-set the bitter tang of the herbs whose aromatic qualities are sought. There is a lavish infusion of herbs in the "red" type which is accordingly strongly sweetened, but although the sweetness is distinctly there, it is evenly balanced by the bitter aroma. In the "white" type the bitter aroma is somewhat reduced, so that there remains some "free" sweetness. In the dry vermouths, where a lesser amount of static sweetness is sought, the aromatic infusion has also to be considerably reduced. The Carpano formula, on the other hand, leaves the sweet-content more or less unchanged, but points towards "dry" with a stronger infusion of bitter aroma. Consequently, Carpano is the most aromatic of all.

Of the ingredients used to-day, angelica, aloes, cinnamon, gentian, orange peel, mint, vanilla, sage, and thyme are the most important, plus absinth blossoms which give the decisive flavour. How it came about that the German word for *artemisia absinthium*: WERMUT, gave its name to the wine is unknown. Possibly it was adopted some time ago to distinguish the wine from the *Absinthe* liqueur which was derived from the leaves of the same plant and is now generally prohibited because of its toxic properties.

The apposite mixture of bitter aromatic herbs is steeped for a considerable time in the properly matured and blended base wine, until the flavours are extracted. Concurrently, part of the miscellany is infused in alcohol, since some of the ingredients are apt to render their flavour more easily and fully in alcohol than in wine. At some stage in the proceedings the desired amount of sugar (most of it caramelized for bitterness) is added, and the alcohol blended with the wine. The finished vermouth reaches a degree of about 17% of alcohol (30° proof)—white vermouth somewhat less, dry vermouth slightly more.

What determines the quality of the resulting vermouth to a great extent is the subsequent process of clarification. It must be pasteurized for keeping. Refrigerating it to about 18 degrees causes the herbal substances to condense, and some seven filtrations in all are needed to clear off the insoluble residue. In between all these operations, the wine needs periods of rest to amalgamate and harmonize its components. Altogether five years go by in the course of production.

Speaking of the refrigerating process reminds me of one particularly gratifying experience I had at Martini's plant near Turin, when I was offered a tumbler full of ice-cold—not vermouth, but that aromatized alcohol infusion I mentioned before. This bitter-sweet, limpid liqueur, coming out from the refrigerator tubes, was the most luxurious drink one could imagine, frightfully strong of course, and I still wonder why no vermouth maker has ever thought of it as a new type of liqueur, instead of producing it only as a vermouth component?

This idea might seem to confirm the English taste in

only table wine in existence which is derived from *passito* grapes.

*   *   *

The wine production of Lombardy does not call for much special attention. Lombardy is, of course, a very large territory and vines are grown in all parts of it, in every village, in the plain as well as on the beautiful hills around the North-Italian lakes. It produces altogether some 2½ to 3 million hectolitres. Most of it is of rather ordinary type, but there are a good deal of acceptable, and some even very good, though unnamed, wines reaching the inns in the provincial towns and the restaurants of Milan. Here, as everywhere, I am all for those light, unpretentious local wines, white or red, which are so pleasant to drink.

One quality of considerable note, however, are the wines of the Valtellina. This is the valley stretching from the northern tip of Lake Como in an easterly direction towards the Stelvio pass, just south of the Spluegen, Maloja, and Bernina, with the town of Sondrio in the centre. Enclosed between mountain ranges of some 10,000 feet, and with the glaciers of the Engadin in its immediate neighbourhood, this is a rather peculiar position for vine-growing.

And yet, the Valtellina produces an excellent red wine. It is all grown on "Nebbiolo" vines, whose grapes, as we have heard already, require a final touch of somewhat harsher weather to achieve perfection. They get plenty of this during harvest time, although in that valley, cut deep between the steep slopes of the mountains, the cold wind of the North blows high above the mountain ranges without touching the vineyards too severely. Once grapes have fully matured, they can withstand a fair amount of frost. During spring and summer, at any rate, they get all the sun they need for growing and ripening on the terraced slopes which face due south.

Grumello, Inferno, Sassella, and *Valgella* are the best species, probably in that order. They are somewhat lighter than the *Nebbiolos* of Piedmont, hardly over 12% of alcohol, possess a more brilliant and much lighter robe, great liveliness and a penetrating bouquet. The *Grumello* accounts for a certain pleasing sweetness of the kind we appreciate in the more robust burgundies.

The name of the valley is usually given only to the white wine of the region. The *Valtellina* is a wine of great repute for its fresh taste; it is light in colour, and moderately alcoholic (some 10 or 11 per cent). Neither the red nor the white Valtellina wines are known to any great extent in England or America, or even in Italy herself: nearly the whole of the production is consigned to Switzerland.

Another Lombardian wine district of some importance is the province of Pavia, which borders on Piedmont. A rather good, light wine comes from there, called *Frecciarossa,* a name one would more readily associate with a red wine. Indeed, there is also a red *Frecciarossa,* dry and smooth, but it lacks distinction. *Barbacarlo* and *Buttafuoco* are two more red wines of this district. The latter, particularly, is distinguished by the brilliance of its colour; but the quality of both is subject to strong fluctuations. Neither of them is very alcoholic, so that the singularly smooth taste of the good vintages easily appears somewhat flat in the poorer years.

More remarkable than the table wines of this district is the *Moscato di Casteggio.* It differs from other *Moscato* growths by its very strong, though not so delicate bouquet. I place it fairly high on my list, just because of this unusual variation. It is produced in a straight and in a sparkling quality.

Still, I maintain that the best wine of Lombardy is the *Petroio,* served in the restaurant *La Tampa* of Milan: a full bodied, dark-red wine, dry and strong—which comes from Tuscany. Incidentally, in Tuscany it is completely unknown, except within the narrow precincts of its actual place of birth. One of those cases, not so very rare in Italy, of a speciality of unusual quality which might have been left undiscovered but for one enterprising man.

*   *   *

When I was a small boy, my father—who flattered himself on being a connoisseur of wines—used to call every sweet or even sweetish wine "a wine for the ladies". Indeed, my mother and my aunts only liked sweet wines and turned up their noses at anything which was even slightly dry. Nowadays connoisseurs still look down on sweet wines, and though they may order one for a woman guest at a restaurant, a sweet wine is not supposed to appeal to a masculine palate. Amazingly enough, most men have a sweet tooth and love eating chocolates, sticky sweet puddings, and the most sugary *gateaux*—but when it comes to drinking they pretend to shudder at sweetness. Any number of good reasons are brought up to rationalize this attitude, but they all boil down to the simple word smart.

The feminine sex are much more reasonable in their eating and drinking habits, it seems to me. When a woman likes wine to be sweet she does not care whether her taste is modern or old fashioned, feminine or not: she enjoys the sweetness in food, and drink, and that is that. Of course, there are quite a number of women who

like dry wines, the drier the better; they are the type
who will gobble up all the olives, the salads and the
cipollatas at a party, and leave the *marons glacés* and the
petits fours. The others, and they are in the majority,
refuse to accept the expert's verdict that sweetness is
undesirable in a wine, and, bless them, get gay and just
a little more talkative in a very sweet way after a glass
or two of sweet wine.

As far as "manly" taste goes, one might take a lesson
from the Romagna. The *Romagnoli* are the most sturdy
race imaginable, tall, broadly built, proud, fierce, and
unshakable. Most of the famous—or ill-famed—condot-
tieri of the years around 1400 came from there, Jacopo
Sforza among others, the peasant boy who by virtue of
dare-devil initiative and on the strength of a handful of
soldiers of similar calibre forged one of the most fearful
armies of his time, and whose son was to become duke
and ruler of Milan and Lombardy.

Nevertheless, the wine that rules the tables of the
Romagna all the way down the "Via Emilia" from
Bologna to Rimini is a light white wine, fresh and strong
in flavour, which is definitely on the sweet side of the
vaguely defined borderland that separates the clearly
sweet wines from the perfectly dry ones. In quality, it
varies enormously from a pleasant, though ordinary,
table wine of "Trebbiano", "Albana", and other grapes,
to some outstandingly good *Albana* vintages, some of
which are glamorous semi-sweet delights, others perfect
dry wines of high class. Unfortunately, you will not find
them farther away from their home than Milan. They
are the stock-in-trade of the nearly one hundred miles-
long string of beach resorts on the Adriatic coast between
Marina di Ravenna and Pesaro-Senigallia. At its southern
end, another wine comes to the fore, too, the *Verdicchio*

di Jesi, a very light, clear, and delicate table wine, slightly tart in taste, but well balanced enough even to have made its appearance in London.

This *Albana* should not be confused with the wine of the Albano hills near Rome. The most famous species is that grown on the hills of Bertinoro, near Cesena. They say that it "embraces the palate", and very fitting this description is. It could not be applied to any other white wine I know, not even to those that are, in their way, even better than this golden wine of the Romagna. *Albana* is, I should say, such a sensuous wine; you feel elated at the mere sight of the first glass, brilliant in the strong light of the cloudless days, and it is one of the very few wines which you want to taste in endless quantity. It is a pity that the people of the Romagna, well-endowed as they are, do not bother to standardize some of the more distinguished of their *Albana* wines, which would make the wine easier to market, especially for export. In the large area between Imola and Sant' Arcangelo di Romagna where the bulk of it is grown, there occur, naturally enough, numerous variations in the quality of the wine, according to the sites and to the training of the vines, so that on the whole the output is somewhat uneven. *Albana* will never be a disappointment, not even in the smallest tavern. The local people certainly know where to obtain the best. But for the sake of its standing with regard to other wines I wish there were some possibility of precise classification to guide a wider public.

If there is anything one can put on a par with the golden glow of *Albana,* it is the pre-eminent wine of the Romagna, the rich, deep red *San Giovese*. One glass of each, and you can have no doubt that the two grow on the same spot.

The *San Giovese* is a wine of very even quality. No praise can be too high for it. Its dryness is free from any trace of sharpness, such as red wines sometimes show. Full of body though it is, it is mellow and warm in taste, as if it were enveloped in a tender veil of sweetness.

For wine lovers, as well as for growers, this tranquil wine with its fragrant bouquet has only one fault: it does not travel. If you want to drink it, you must go to Bologna—which is worth a visit, anyway—or to one of the smaller towns of the Romagna. The *San Giovese* alone will repay the expense.

Usually only wines of low alcoholic degree are subject to deterioration under conditions of transport, so this should not be the case with *San Giovese*. For a red wine it is indeed not highly alcoholic, between 11 and 12%, rarely reaching thirteen. However, that is about the level of *Chianti* and the red wines of Verona, and those travel very well. It may be rather the density of the *San Giovese,* so pleasant to the palate, which upsets its poise when it has to travel too far, or more likely some still unidentified chemical influences coming from the composition of the soil. There is little doubt, however, that these chemical elements could be, if not actually eliminated, at least rendered harmless by appropriate treatment.

The *San Giovese* well deserves the care and trouble that would be necessary to enable it to compete on foreign markets with other better known, but hardly superior wines. But if the *San Giovese* does not travel, it has a remarkable ability of migrating! Just on the other side of the Apennines, in Tuscany, the "San Giovese" vine has established itself as providing the basic component of the more energetic *Chianti*. And if *Chianti* has been such a success with the international public, the *San Giovese* should be even more so.

In the western stretch of the "Via Emilia", at Parma and Modena, another red wine is strongly featured and very popular: *Lambrusco*. Personally, I do not think it has very much to recommend it, except a certain curiosity value, insofar as it is an effervescent dry table wine, and I must admit that it goes very well with the extremely rich food of the district. However, I find even the best *Lambrusco* growth, that of Sorbara, too harsh for my taste.

I lived in the Romagna long enough to know the country and its people fairly well. Somehow or other, I felt quite at home the moment I arrived. It is, probably, everybody's boundless hospitality, and also a certain friendliness in the landscape itself—in a way you feel you belong to the Romagna as soon as you have unpacked your things. Your neighbours are friendly and helpful. Everything is in a proportion which one can cope with, close at hand, easy and simple.

Neither the towns (with the exception of Bologna) nor the countryside—these Apennine foothills flattening out into the wide plain of the Po—are particularly beautiful in the usual picture-postcard sense. It is the very richness of that country of soft hills and endless fields, neatly intersected with low hedges and rows of mulberry and fruit trees, that creates a peculiar sort of aesthetic emotion . . . the feel of beauty more than its visual expression. Every inch of terrain, every leaf, breathes fertility. Indeed, by means of skilful planning and with the generous help of nature (the wheat crop is brought in by mid-June) one cornfield may also successively yield pumkins, lupine, clover, and maize, plus the fruit and the grapes from the trees and vines that flank it, and occasionally even cross it.

No wonder that these people eat well, drink well, live well—and insist on living well. Even American troops stood gasping at the abundance of food in farmhouses that were half destroyed by gun fire. Never before in their lives had they seen such succulent dishes.

The *Romagnoli* know how to get the last touch of enjoyment out of every occasion in life. They have made a fine art of combining work with pleasure. I used to know a long-distance lorry driver who carried a demijohn of wine fastened to the top of his cabin. A rubber hose with plug led to his seat, arranged so handily that he could sip a mouthful of wine now and then without stopping his driving. It goes without saying that he knew what he did, could stand what he drank, was never drunk and never had an accident. But he had a jolly good time on his journeys.

One of my most amusing recollections is that of an alfresco dinner a friend of mine arranged for me at his apricot and peach plantation, a short way from Cesena. Antoniacci was, and I hope still is, a comfortably plump man whose passionate interest in his dozen or so pigs can only be compared with the devotion some Englishmen have towards their gardens. The whole thing really started with a discussion on what was more important to human happiness and well-being, the pig or the olive? In Italy, the pig not only gives bacon and ham. The pork sausage in its various forms is the staple food all the year round, and with "cooking fat" happily absent, lard is the only alternative to olive oil.

That was more or less my friend's argument. But, if I remember well, I—who am very partial to olives, black and green—won the discussion with the contention that the olive was more important because pigs come to their prime (which is about 420 pounds in Italy) through a final stage of feeding with the caked residues of oil pressing. I don't think either of us, perhaps was perfectly sober at the time we started on the discussion, nor were the company that listened to us, but possibly the argument was not much sillier than a television game. Anyway, the prize so to speak, of the discussion—the dinner given by Antoniacci—more than justified it.

Five of us sat around a table set under the loaded trees of his orchard, with the manageress of the plantation acting as hostess. The hills in the distance were enamelled with sunset, Gina was a pretty girl of twenty-three or four, and after the customary introduction of salame and raw ham with melons that had been hung in the well-shaft for cooling, she brought out that indispensable Italian dish of heaped noodles—with ragout of chicken livers that spoke well for what was to come after. I had to wait a little for the next course, for I ate just one plate of *tagliatelle*, the other men two, Gina three. Indeed, the next course was grilled *escalopes* of veal, followed by chicken grilled on an open wood fire, and there were ten chickens—two for each of us.

Even the gastronomic experience I had previously had in the Romagna had not trained me sufficiently for food on such a scale, nor was the constant flow of *Albana* of any further help towards this last effort. Half of my second chicken remained on the serving dish. And with a glance requesting my consent, Gina helped herself and finished it off with appetite and enjoyment.

"Tell me", I asked her, "if I had left a whole chicken instead of only half, could you have eaten it as well?" —"Of course", she said, "and a third". I am sure she meant it, and the point really is she was neither very big nor plump, just a healthy, buxom girl with a good day's work behind her, who was enjoying herself, and wanted to eat well for the pleasure of it.

Alas! not all of my memories of the Romagna are as easy and carefree as that. But even those experiences which had a rougher side, were never quite without some happy reward.

It was not much later that, while on a mission of partisan-liaison in a period of shifting attacks and counter-attacks, I found myself suddenly cut-off with two companions. There was nothing we could do but seek shelter. In near-darkness, we found our way into an almost deserted small town and entered a bomb-scarred house. Next morning, the situation was unchanged, and exploring the house we found some flour in the pantry, a side of bacon and even a few jars of home-made jam. And, looking out of from the window, we saw a variety of vegetables growing at the end of the garden—although these were not of much use to us, as we dared not venture out of the house. There were occasional German patrols about, and we thought we had better not risk being seen. The prospect of the days in front of us was far from promising. How many would there be? One? Two? Thirty? We had no means of telling.

However, three men shut in a large house cannot sit still all day long. We explored. We were discreet about writing-cabinets and personal belongings, but otherwise fairly thorough. Of course, we had the excuse that we might find something more to eat tucked away in some less obvious place of storage, but mainly, I think, we searched in order to kill time and to have something to do. Everything in the house suggested the fairly orderly departure of the owners after the bomb had exploded in the courtyard and ripped the walls of the house open.

We could not even find blankets, and were obliged to use curtains in their place.

Unfortunately, the cellar which we had hoped to explore turned out to be inaccessible, for what appeared to be its entrance was blocked by a heap of rubble from the tumbled walls. Finally, we advanced to the loft, and there, to our great surprise, we found something not usually connected with the space under the roof: rows and rows of bottles of old wines, neatly packed in straw, with handwritten labels indicating the years of vintage —all early 1900s—the grapes, and the sites of the vineyards.

I still do not know, and certainly shall never learn, why the owner "cellared" his wines in the attic. At any rate they were all what the Italians call *Vin Santo*, which does not mean to say "holy wine" but: "Wine for the Saints". Saints we were not, but we were not slow in broaching the bottles and our immediate future at once looked a lot brighter. Needless to say, we passed the days, sharing out what food we had, in a state of gentle inebriation—gentle, because we had to be careful not to make any noise. Indeed, we were almost sad when after a time we spied a patrol in Allied uniform from our window. We were free to leave our not-too-safe shelter. It also meant that we had to abandon the tender solace of our glorious treasure. I still think gratefully of its rightful owner's unintentional, but nevertheless divine, hospitality.

Nearly all of what is known as *Vin Santo* is produced by small individual growers, from *uva passita*. Very little of it comes up for sale; it is held as a wine to make a gift of, not a profit.

Indeed, *Vin Santo* is a very noble wine, and one might say almost a work of art. The grapes are not chosen—as they are for other *passito* wines—on account of their sweetness (which by itself makes for easier drying, but tends to flatten the aroma) but with regard to strong flavour. Consequently, to allow the air to circulate around them more freely, the grapes are not spread on racks as is usual, but hung up on long strings to which they are fastened by their stems, one bunch beneath the other. This is a rather tricky little job, and it is easy to understand that it cannot be done with sizeable quantities of grapes.

Only in our time some of the bigger growers worked out a somewhat simplified method by hanging the grapes on strong zinc-wires which are fitted with hooks. The most notable of these are the *Chianti* producers of Tuscany whose white "Trebbiano" and "Malvasia" grapes are ideally suited for making this special wine. But even this "commercial" production is rather limited.

The general idea is to obtain a dessert wine of very high alcoholic degree and comparatively low sweet content: one in which the sweetness of the wine is, so to speak, fully covered by its strength. *Vin Santo* attains an alcoholic degree of 16% (28° proof spirit), against only 7% sweet content. If you compare this with the proportion between alcohol and sugar in other dessert wines, you will see that the balance here is tipped strongly in favour of the content of alcohol. To some extent, the phenomenon of this unusual ratio is also influenced by letting the wine mature "in wood" for several years before it is bottled.

In autumn, every good housewife in the Romagna is busy fastening grapes on strings, just as the growers do. She hangs them up under the stairs perhaps, or in the loft, wherever she finds a dry and airy place. These grapes, though, are for eating, as a sweet dessert fruit.

By mid-winter they are ready, although not as dry as the Malaga grapes we know; roughly one third of the juice, very thick and sweet, is still left in them. They are really delicious, and do not taste like dried fruit but more like fresh grapes of a kind you have not tasted before.

"Opening day" is the First of January, and a plate of *uva passita* is *de rigueur* at the end of every New Year's lunch. Every family makes a point of finding out in advance whether any of their friends—prevented perhaps by lack of suitable space, or lack of time—have failed to make their own dried grapes. And who have not done so, will certainly receive a gift of a bunch or two from all their friends on New Year's morning. This is extremely important, because to eat *uva passita* on New Year's Day ensures that those who do so will never run short of money in the coming year. And who would not wish his friends to be well off?

XII

In Italy, cooking with wine is nothing like as popular as it is in France. Though some of the exquisite Italian specialities may not be of much use to us, there are a few things of note with which we may like to enrich our cuisine.

It is all very well for the Italian farmer to sprinkle their minced meat lavishly with wine and *grappa* when they prepare their *salami*. But I doubt if we could induce our sausage-makers to do the same, though it certainly enhances the taste. And the Venetian custom of cooking artichokes in wine, simple as it is, loses much of its attraction, even for determined gourmets, if they have to bear in mind how much the cheapest wine costs. In Venice, with its abundance of local wines, it is quite a different proposition; still, cooking them slowly and lovingly in wine is the most beautiful way of preparing artichokes.

More realistic is the idea of giving meat sauces and soups a final dash of wine. A spoonful or two—white or red, according to whether the sauce is light or dark— added at the last moment, just before serving it, will do much to improve any sauce or soup. Your inspirations as to which wines to combine with your sauces can be quite bold; even vermouth can occasionally be used in cooking. Of course, the wine should not overpower the natural taste of your dish. It should add its aroma, no more.

In the following recipe it is the sauce that "makes" your steak, and though I have only come across this dish in the house of friends in Rome and nowhere else

I call it an Italian recipe because my hostess called it BISTECCA PAOLINA—after her cook.

Buy the best steak, preferably fillet. Have it cut half an inch thick, and trimmed free from the fat and gristle which your butcher—contrary to you—may consider as belonging to the steak. You will also need some fresh parsley, an onion or two, some French mustard, and some red wine: not the cheapest, please. First, finely cut a tablespoonful of parsley for each steak. Then chop about a teaspoonful of onion per steak. Put both in a bowl and add a teaspoonful of French mustard and a small glass of red wine for each: stir this intriguing mixture well.

You can now fry your steaks, seasoned as you please, in very little oil, or fat, exactly to your liking—well done, under-done, three-quarters raw, just as you always do it. At the moment when your steaks are ready, pour the contents of the bowl over them into the pan. Do not get a shock if the mixture steams and sizzles like mad—I have made these steaks a hundred times and always think something has gone wrong at this moment—but do as I do, turn the steaks over once, stir the sauce with a wooden spoon, and serve immediately. The onions and the parsley should not be cooked; just heated!

A recipe I have enjoyed fairly frequently in restaurants and in the homes of my friends in different parts of Italy, is an OMELETTE WITH KIDNEYS. Gently cook some chopped onion, parsley, and finely cut mushrooms in butter or oil. After a few minutes, add a little stock and about three times the amount red wine, and let it cook vigorously for a few minutes. While your sauce is bubbling happily, take another frying pan and fry some finely sliced kidneys; add the kidneys to the sauce which must now only simmer until the kidneys are cooked. As soon as the kidneys have settled in the wine-sauce, start on your omelette, and fill it with the mixture which is seasoned with salt and pepper at the very last moment. This makes an excellent substantial entrée, or, served with French beans or young peas, a good main dish.

CHICKEN A LA MARENGO is an impressive dish which can give your guests the idea that you are quite an outstanding cook, though it is really fairly easy to make. It is best done with very young chickens, but if you are stuck with a middle-aged fowl double the cooking time and you should be all right and your bird tender. Ask your butcher to cut your chicken in four pieces. Season, and fry quickly in hot oil. Cook some chopped shallots in butter, add some quartered mushrooms, stock, tomato *purée,* and finally a large wineglassful of dry white wine. Pour the sauce over your chicken, and braise slowly for half an hour. A very spectacular way to garnish the dish is with eggs poached in oil. If you are conscious of your figure, you can of course poach the eggs in water.

Probably the most popular of Italian wine dishes is a variation of ZABAIONE—normally a drink of wine and eggs— prepared as a sweet: one yolk of egg per person is creamed with one ounce of sugar in a small frying pan, then put over a low heat and beaten with a fork; care must be taken that it does not start to set: it must remain creamy! When hot, one eggcupful of *Marsala* for every egg used, is poured over the mixture, and it is allowed to heat through again, beaten all the time. Mind your fingers!

I also like very much the French equivalent to *Zabaione*: CHAUDEAU ("hot water"), made with ordinary table wine. Any cheap wine will do, except the so-called "cooking wines". Red wine may be used as well as white ones, but a white wine gives a nicer colour.

If I say it is my favourite, the fact that it is very easy and quick to prepare may have something to do with it. First, cream the yolks of six eggs with 10 to 11 ounces of sugar (it depends on whether your wine is slightly sweet or not) in a large bowl, then add slowly—constantly beating—half a bottle of wine, and add three cloves. Meanwhile bring some water to the boil in a saucepan. Now put the bowl into the pan so that it is partly immersed in the water which is kept boiling all the time. Let the *Chaudeau* heat, beating continuously until it is all foamy. It must rise, but not boil; the flatter the bowl, the easier it is to beat the mixture to a foam. Serve hot, immediately, with sponge or chocolate fingers.

Your guests will have to wait while you make the *Chaudeau*: there is no way out of this. The only thing you can prepare in advance is the egg-sugar cream, without, however, adding the wine. The creaming takes a little while, because the mixture should be very smooth. The wine must be added last thing just before heating the cream, but this does not take very long.

Of course wine goes very well with fruit, and the Italians have long discovered that fruit which is allowed to lie in wine absorbs the flavour of the wine and blends it beautifully with its own. A semi-sweet, aromatic white wine, *Frascati* for instance, will enhance any fruit salad. The smaller you cut your fruit, the easier the wine can do its work, but allow it an hour or two in your refrigerator to do its best. And if you can spare a glass of brandy . . .

In Italy, it is almost the rule to serve strawberries with a generous sprinkling of *Marsala* or *Albana*. The wine is added just before serving.

There is no getting away from the fact that the following recipe is a little involved and on the expensive side. DOLCE DI FRUTTA is the sweet to serve for very special occasions, to friends you particularly cherish.

Beat ½ pint cream, 2 yolks, 1 whole egg, 2 ounces sugar, and a small pod of vanilla in the *Bain Marie* or over steam till it has a creamy consistency. Let it cool and then mix well with 1 gill of whipped cream and a little previously dissolved gelatine. Line your deepest glass dish with fruit, either strawberries or sliced oranges, tinned apricots or peaches. Put a layer of sponge fingers steeped in sweet white wine over the fruit, cover with the cream, and go on adding layers of fruit, sponge fingers and cream alternately until your dish is full. Top with a layer of fruit and garnish with whipped cream. Leave in the refrigerator until ready to serve.

*   *   *

Under modern building conditions, it is not so easy to obtain the temperature a wine needs as it was at a time when a well-built cellar was a matter of course in every house. With one or two exceptions, natural cellar temperature is just the right thing to make white wines fit to come to your table, preferably presented in a bucket of ice to give them that final touch of chill. Few people however, and I am not myself among those few, know with precision exactly how much time a wine requires for cooling in a refrigerator.

There is, I am afraid, no precise guidance on the proper relationship between wine and a refrigerator. The two belong to different worlds that must be reconciled individually. One is prone either to under-estimate the time a refrigerator requires for doing the job, or to overdo it: so much depends on the temperature of the wine at the moment of putting it in. Everybody has to try to arrive at his own conclusion by a system of trial and error.

One cannot measure the temperature inside a bottle. If you touch the bottle it may feel quite cold, while the wine itself is far from being ready. However, a white table wine should not be over-cooled either; those with a very delicate bouquet might easily come to harm. 50° Fahrenheit is about the right thing—half way, that is, between freezing point and room temperature. The very dry wines come out better at a somewhat lower point than the medium-dry varieties. Sparkling wines of course must be very nearly "iced".

As we have to put up with shallow cellars—if any—which also house hot water pipes and boilers, we must at least keep the wine as far away as possible from sources of heat, and from the sunny side, away from light, and in a dry, reasonably airy place. Again, the right temperature for storing all wines lies around 50° Fahrenheit. It does not matter if this level changes by a few degrees during winter and summer, but strong changes of temperature can easily put wine out of condition. Red wines will suffer more than white if the place is too cold, and vice versa.

Red wines, of course, are served *chambrée*: at room temperature. The wine must be allowed quite a few hours of slow conditioning towards its ideal serving temperature of some 68 degrees. Placing the cellar-cold bottles near a fire or on a hot-plate, is almost criminal.

Sweet dessert wines may not necessarily require such an accurate temperature as white table wines, but I think most, if not all of them, definitely gain when they are served fairly fresh. After all, we also ice our cocktails. I even prefer a red sweet wine to be fairly cool rather than *chambrée,* though I am prepared to admit that this is a controversial statement.

What is really sinful in these isles is the treatment given to *apéritives.* By implication we admit that an *apéritif* ought to be iced, in so far as we put a piece of ice into the glass. If the sherry, or vermouth, is being kept at its proper temperature, that is 32°, the ice will keep the drink cool while we hold it. But very few bar-tenders, very few of the very good clubs even, keep the wine as it ought to be kept. Of course, warmish wine cannot be cooled in a minute by that poor floating piece of ice, and simply dissolves it. The effect is a drink that is not iced, but watered! Vermouth, even more than sherry, should be really ice-cool.

Just as important as the right temperature, is the proper affinity between wine and food. The time of the nobles (also English noblemen—not only French and Italians!) who spent their lives singling out those wines which were best to accompany each of the many artful products of their cooks, has gone for good. What remains to us is to realize the broad outlines of the intricate relationship between wine and food: the general pattern is that strongly seasoned dishes require wines with a more pronounced aroma and greater vinosity—delicate dishes, a wine with a more gentle approach. If only one wine is served during a meal, it is wiser to choose one with not too marked a personality. Otherwise, white should precede red, dry should come before sweet, a lighter wine before the more alcoholic ones.

This scheme is in line with the general idea of serving the heavier richer dishes after the lighter ones. But one has to appreciate the many exceptions to these rules:

e.g., the *apéritif* is usually the heaviest of all; sparkling wines are always lighter than the table wines they follow; most dessert wines are white and yet do not interfere with the red wines served during the meal. I would even point to an intriguing variation in the *apéritif*/wine sequence: after a dry sherry, introducing the meal with a *demi-sec* wine brings a subtle nuance before going on to the dry red wines with the main course. After a vermouth (Martini style or plain) the standard sequence: dry white/dry red is better.

There is much to be said for decanting wines. The "airing" of the wine may indeed be to its advantage. I myself however am not in favour of using decanters. I prefer the sight of the original bottle which so pleasantly recalls the idea of the silent shadows of cool wine-cellars, the vinous scent emanating from those dim ranges of casks and bottles in their quiet confine. Nor am I quite so sure if it is the right thing to disturb the wine before pouring it into glasses, and the airing is achieved in any case if one opens the bottles (replacing the corks not too tightly) some time, say an hour or so, before serving the wine.

The custom of decanting is probably derived from the time when bottles as we know them were not yet in use and all wine was kept in barrels. If you have some of these sparkling crystal flasks, use them by all means. They are charming to look at! At any rate, decanting a wine does away with the possibility that any unsightly sediment may find its way into the glass when the wine is being poured out. However, better technical methods of filtering and clearing wines before they are bottled have cut down the occurrence of sediment to a very great extent, by comparison with what it was only fifty years ago.

It is true that sediment is unsightly when it occurs. But it does not indicate—as many people believe—that the wine is out of condition. The more body (which is only another word for the technical term "viscosity') a wine has, and the older it is, the greater its tendency to condense and segregate the less soluble particles. Some old red wines go so far as to form a slight film on the inner surface of the bottle, a "shirt" as the Italians say. It has to be understood that wine is a living thing, and goes on living after it has been put into bottles. The term "well-aged wine" actually indicates that some natural process, by which its quality steadily improves, is continuously going on in the wine long after it has fermented and properly matured.

Apart from the often neglected necessity of changing glasses with the wines, I am not particular about glasses. A hearty wine can stand a fairly thick glass. I like the present vogue of the very thin, tulip-shaped glasses better than the goblets of the recent past because they hold the bouquet of the wine; they are also so thin and light that their touch on the lips is hardly noticeable. But those now old-fashioned, more V-shaped glasses with their hidden fires and intricate sparkles in the honeycombed diamonds of their cut glass are a fascinating sight on the table, and seem to add to the magical attraction of the wine they hold.

In spite of the obvious snags attached to most storing facilities, it is still worse to order wines at the very last minute. Wines should rest for at least a week, or even a fortnight, after delivery.

It is perhaps not so easy to say what wines one should store. Considering the average taste (as far as such a thing exists) and taking into account what Italian wines are available over here, I should think that those of

Verona are probably the most reliable choice to start with. Some six bottles of *Soave*, six of either *Bardolino* or *Valpolicella*, and half a dozen *Chiaretto* would be a good basis from which to venture further into the wider field of Italian wines, and decide what to take up and what not. Some bottles of *Barolo* should be included for choice occasions, and a few *Barbera* ought to be in store to represent the more robust line of Piedmont.

Regarding the wines of Tuscany, it takes a little enterprise and insistence to find a supplier for the fairly scarce vintage *Chiantis* (in bottles, not in flasks), but they are definitely worth the trouble and a very good buy at the price at present asked for them. *Vin Santo* of excellent vintage is also available and its price not excessive, In the sweeter line of dessert wines, *Moscato Passito d'Asti* is sure to please you; as to the others, this is again a matter of trying those one likes best.

To drink wine is an uneasy compromise between the desire to enjoy more of it and the implication that you miss its taste as soon as it goes to your head. Wine is a placid companion; it gives a healthy satisfaction to our senses, but to enjoy its delights we must not dull them with too much of the alcohol. With wine one must exercise a discriminating—I should almost say, artistic—taste.

We shall be nearer to the easy understanding of wine that belongs to those people who lovingly tend its growth, if we do it the honour of the appreciation it deserves. Let wine come to our tables; we need it as we need our dearest friends. It will remind us of the sunshine that is caught in the glass we hold, of happy days, of tender evenings spent in the country where it grew.

Better still, the wine may help us to find our way there
again!

> " . . . whoever is my friend
> And at my table dines
> Shall join in drinking at the end
> The toast of ABSENT WINES".

(Colin Ellis).

INDEX

Aglianico, 44
Albana, 100–101, 105, 113
Aleatico, 46
Apéritifs, 55
Arbia, 20
Asti Spumante, 69, 74–76, 84

Barbacarlo, 98
Barbaresco, 79–81
Barbera, 12, 77, 82, 119
Bardolino, 24, 119
Barolo, 16, 77–81, 119
Blauburgunder, 32
Bonarda, 83
Borgogna Nera, 32
Brachetto, 83
Brandy, 35, 48, 52, 54, 113
Brunello, 21
Buttafuoco, 98

Caluso, 85
Cannellino, 58
Capri, 63–64
Carema, 81
Castel del Monte, 44
Castelli Romani, 58–60, 62
Cerasuolo, 60
Cesanese del Piglio, 60
Chianti, 15, 17–24, 26, 62, 75, 102, 108, 119
Chiaretto, 26–27, 119
Cinque Terre, 96
Cirò, 44
Colli Albani, 58

Colli Euganei, 28
Colli Lanuviani, 58
Colli Trevigliani, 28
Colonna, 58
Coronata, 95
Cortese, 84

Dolceacqua, 95
Dolcetto, 77–78

Eloro, 44
Est Est Est, 61–62
Etna, 40

Falerno, 63–65
Faro, 43
Fernet, 54
Fiano di Avellino, 63
Frappato di Vittoria, 47
Frascati, 57–61, 113
Frecciarossa, 98
Freisa, 92, 93

Garganega, 28
Gattinara, 81
Gewuerztraminer, 33
Girò, 46
Gragnano, 65, 67
Grappa, 54, 110
Grappa Ruta, 54
Greco, 47
Greco di Tuffo, 63
Grignolino, 83
Grumello, 98

121

Inferno, 98
Italian Gin, 88

Kalterer, 33
Kuechelberger, 35

Lacrima Castrovillari, 44
Lacrima Christi, 63–64
Lagarino, 33
Lambrusco, 103
Liqueurs, 53

Malvasia, 44–45, 59–60
Mamertino, 43
Marino, 58
Marsala, 48–51, 112–113
Marsaluovo, 51
Martina Franca, 44
Merlot, 32
Monica, 46
Montecarlo, 21
Montepulciano, 21
Moscatello, 36
Moscato, 34–36, 38, 45, 69–70,
    74–76, 84–85
Moscato Passito, 35, 119

Nasco, 52–53
Nebbiolo, 80–81, 98
Nuragus, 44–45

Oliena, 51
Orvieto, 62, 75

Passito di Siracusa, 38
Petroio, 99
Pinot Nero, 32
Polcevera, 95

Prosecco, 29

Ravello, 63
Recioto, 27
Roccese, 96

Salento, 38
San Giovese, 101–103
San Severo, 44
Santa Maddalena, 32
Santo Stefano, 44
Sassella, 98
Savignon, 13
Savuto, 43–44
Sciacchetrà, 96
Silvaner, 33
Soave, 16, 22–23, 25, 119
Solopaca, 63
Spumante, 36, 69, 71–72, 74–
    77, 85

Terlano, 32
Torre Giulia, 44
Traminer, 33
Trebbiano, 28

Valgella, 98
Valpantena, 24
Valpolicella, 24, 119
Valtellina, 98
Velletri, 58
Verdicchio di Jesi, 101
Vermentino, 45, 95
Vermouth, 34, 46, 49, 55, 77–
    78, 86–93, 110, 116
Vernaccia, 44–45
Vesuvio, 64
Vino Veronese, 28
Vin Santo, 35, 107–108, 119

A CATALOGUE OF SELECTED DOVER BOOKS
IN ALL FIELDS OF INTEREST

A CATALOGUE OF SELECTED DOVER BOOKS
IN ALL FIELDS OF INTEREST

AMERICA'S OLD MASTERS, James T. Flexner. Four men emerged unexpectedly from provincial 18th century America to leadership in European art: Benjamin West, J. S. Copley, C. R. Peale, Gilbert Stuart. Brilliant coverage of lives and contributions. Revised, 1967 edition. 69 plates. 365pp. of text.

21806-6 Paperbound $3.00

FIRST FLOWERS OF OUR WILDERNESS: AMERICAN PAINTING, THE COLONIAL PERIOD, James T. Flexner. Painters, and regional painting traditions from earliest Colonial times up to the emergence of Copley, West and Peale Sr., Foster, Gustavus Hesselius, Feke, John Smibert and many anonymous painters in the primitive manner. Engaging presentation, with 162 illustrations. xxii + 368pp.

22180-6 Paperbound $3.50

THE LIGHT OF DISTANT SKIES: AMERICAN PAINTING, 1760-1835, James T. Flexner. The great generation of early American painters goes to Europe to learn and to teach: West, Copley, Gilbert Stuart and others. Allston, Trumbull, Morse; also contemporary American painters—primitives, derivatives, academics—who remained in America. 102 illustrations. xiii + 306pp.

22179-2 Paperbound $3.00

A HISTORY OF THE RISE AND PROGRESS OF THE ARTS OF DESIGN IN THE UNITED STATES, William Dunlap. Much the richest mine of information on early American painters, sculptors, architects, engravers, miniaturists, etc. The only source of information for scores of artists, the major primary source for many others. Unabridged reprint of rare original 1834 edition, with new introduction by James T. Flexner, and 394 new illustrations. Edited by Rita Weiss. 6⅝ x 9⅝.

21695-0, 21696-9, 21697-7 Three volumes, Paperbound $13.50

EPOCHS OF CHINESE AND JAPANESE ART, Ernest F. Fenollosa. From primitive Chinese art to the 20th century, thorough history, explanation of every important art period and form, including Japanese woodcuts; main stress on China and Japan, but Tibet, Korea also included. Still unexcelled for its detailed, rich coverage of cultural background, aesthetic elements, diffusion studies, particularly of the historical period. 2nd, 1913 edition. 242 illustrations. lii + 439pp. of text.

20364-6, 20365-4 Two volumes, Paperbound $6.00

THE GENTLE ART OF MAKING ENEMIES, James A. M. Whistler. Greatest wit of his day deflates Oscar Wilde, Ruskin, Swinburne; strikes back at inane critics, exhibitions, art journalism; aesthetics of impressionist revolution in most striking form. Highly readable classic by great painter. Reproduction of edition designed by Whistler. Introduction by Alfred Werner. xxxvi + 334pp.

21875-9 Paperbound $2.50

MATHEMATICAL PUZZLES FOR BEGINNERS AND ENTHUSIASTS, Geoffrey Mott-Smith. 189 puzzles from easy to difficult—involving arithmetic, logic, algebra, properties of digits, probability, etc.—for enjoyment and mental stimulus. Explanation of mathematical principles behind the puzzles. 135 illustrations. viii + 248pp.

20198-8 Paperbound $1.75

PAPER FOLDING FOR BEGINNERS, William D. Murray and Francis J. Rigney. Easiest book on the market, clearest instructions on making interesting, beautiful origami. Sail boats, cups, roosters, frogs that move legs, bonbon boxes, standing birds, etc. 40 projects; more than 275 diagrams and photographs. 94pp.

20713-7 Paperbound $1.00

TRICKS AND GAMES ON THE POOL TABLE, Fred Herrmann. 79 tricks and games— some solitaires, some for two or more players, some competitive games—to entertain you between formal games. Mystifying shots and throws, unusual caroms, tricks involving such props as cork, coins, a hat, etc. Formerly *Fun on the Pool Table.* 77 figures. 95pp.

21814-7 Paperbound $1.00

HAND SHADOWS TO BE THROWN UPON THE WALL: A SERIES OF NOVEL AND AMUSING FIGURES FORMED BY THE HAND, Henry Bursill. Delightful picturebook from great-grandfather's day shows how to make 18 different hand shadows: a bird that flies, duck that quacks, dog that wags his tail, camel, goose, deer, boy, turtle, etc. Only book of its sort. vi + 33pp. 6½ x 9¼. 21779-5 Paperbound $1.00

WHITTLING AND WOODCARVING, E. J. Tangerman. 18th printing of best book on market. "If you can cut a potato you can carve" toys and puzzles, chains, chessmen, caricatures, masks, frames, woodcut blocks, surface patterns, much more. Information on tools, woods, techniques. Also goes into serious wood sculpture from Middle Ages to present, East and West. 464 photos, figures. x + 293pp.

20965-2 Paperbound $2.00

HISTORY OF PHILOSOPHY, Julián Marias. Possibly the clearest, most easily followed, best planned, most useful one-volume history of philosophy on the market; neither skimpy nor overfull. Full details on system of every major philosopher and dozens of less important thinkers from pre-Socratics up to Existentialism and later. Strong on many European figures usually omitted. Has gone through dozens of editions in Europe. 1966 edition, translated by Stanley Appelbaum and Clarence Strowbridge. xviii + 505pp. 21739-6 Paperbound $3.00

YOGA: A SCIENTIFIC EVALUATION, Kovoor T. Behanan. Scientific but non-technical study of physiological results of yoga exercises; done under auspices of Yale U. Relations to Indian thought, to psychoanalysis, etc. 16 photos. xxiii + 270pp.

20505-3 Paperbound $2.50

Prices subject to change without notice.
Available at your book dealer or write for free catalogue to Dept. GI, Dover Publications, Inc., 180 Varick St., N. Y., N. Y. 10014. Dover publishes more than 150 books each year on science, elementary and advanced mathematics, biology, music, art, literary history, social sciences and other areas.